KU-021-845

ELIZABETH TAYLOR

THE ILLUSTRATED BIOGRAPHY

ELIZABETH TAYLOR

THE ILLUSTRATED BIOGRAPHY

JAMES CHRISTOPHER

ANDRE
DEUTSCH

www.vci.co.uk

ANDRE
DEUTSCH

First published in Great Britain in 1999 by
André Deutsch Ltd
76 Dean Street
London W1V 5HA

Text copyright © **James Christopher 1999**
Design copyright © **Essential 1999**

Design: **Neal Townsend** for **Essential**
Picture research: **Odile Schmitz** for **Essential**

The right of James Christopher to be identified
as the author of this work has been asserted by
him in accordance with the Copyright, Designs
and Patents Act 1988.

1 3 5 7 9 10 8 6 4 2

All rights reserved. This book is sold subject to
the condition that it may not be reproduced,
stored in a retrieval system, or transmitted, in
any form or by any means, electronic,
mechanical, photocopying, recording or
otherwise, without the publisher's prior
consent.

Printed in **Italy** by **G.E.P. S.p.A.**

A catalogue record for this book is available
from the British Library.

ISBN 0-233-99620-6

For Dina and Clare

Elizabeth

CONTENTS

LIZ: THE SIMPLE TRUTH

Elizabeth Taylor has not made a film that people might want to remember for some years now. In fact, it's been decades since she was known first and foremost as a film actress. Yet she continues to exert a grip on the public's imagination that belies anything she ever did on the silver screen. The simple truth about Taylor is that her greatest role has been her own life story. She is the most glamorous product of a certain era of Hollywood movies whose matinée idols wore their charisma like royalty and their star status under sable furs. Like Diana, the late Princess of Wales, Taylor is an icon. She is impossible to fathom, yet we still seem to know every wrinkle of her life intimately.

For about as long as I can remember, Elizabeth Taylor's life has been one of quite extraordinary excess. Her legendary love affairs, her doomed marriages, her diamonds as big as the Ritz, her several addictions and the soap opera of her health have all been with us for as long as the H-bomb. And to my Catholic parents in the 1960s, inflamed by even more conservatively minded Irish newspapers, Liz was just as lethal.

Before excess became not only fashionable for film stars but the norm, her lifestyle was presented to me as a kind of moral health warning. The *National Velvet* heroine of my childhood was hooked on prescription drugs, she threatened marriages, frittered away fortunes and was sometimes impossible to work with. Yet this roll-call of infamy simply made the scarlet star with the violet eyes appear far more fascinating and complex to me, and millions like me. Elizabeth Taylor was ultimately the forbidden fruit.

A rare moment of calm: Liz and Richard Burton share a moment of peace despite the fact that they were never able to shake off the ever-present paparazzi

Liz's cherished pooch: one of the reasons why Liz does not frequent Britain more often is the strict quarantine laws that prevent her from bringing over her pets

For an impressionable youth growing up in Dublin with little wit and even less pocket-money, hers was clearly a lifestyle to which one might aspire. Even when she started sporting those haystack beehives modelled on Frankenstein's bride, and her heavy figure became a pincushion of diamonds, Elizabeth Taylor still epitomized the unobtainable, overblown glamour of the star juggernaut. And she became more so than ever when everyone from the royals to street cleaners played judge and jury to the latest twists in her rocky marriages and her still shakier affairs. Even the prudish were not immune to this.

From the 1950s to the 1970s, every woman on the planet wanted to look like Elizabeth Taylor, and every man wanted to sleep with her. People took great pleasure in either championing her cause or condemning her – and frequently both. Although Liz was larger than life, she was not beyond the voyeuristic jurisdiction of her massive public. Liz was a Queen of Hearts long before Diana was a twinkle in Earl Spencer's eye. The reason for this is because the studios, particularly MGM, gave her ample opportunity, perhaps even encouraged her from her earliest films, to relive in her daily life what she had been through on celluloid. The way her movie roles shadowed her life, and vice versa, was not only spooky, but at times unhealthy. For long periods of her career she didn't seem to know where her films ended and real life began. Unlike Vivien Leigh, who suffered from similar delusions and was finally tipped into madness by *A Streetcar Named Desire*, Taylor's sanity has held, against all the odds. Even now, after her multiple incarnations as gay icon, perfume magnate, Republican senator's wife, official friend of Michael Jackson and vociferous Aids and cancer campaigner, she continues to haunt the most unlikely and bizarre corners of our lives.

When Swissair Flight 111 plunged into the Atlantic off Nova Scotia in September 1998, with the tragic loss of all 229 passengers and crew, the shadowy fingerprints of yet another Taylor mystery could be discerned. Among the missing artefacts was a multi-million dollar cargo of diamonds, weighing 4.5 pounds, along with 110 pounds of banknotes in transit from an American to a Swiss bank, and an original Picasso painting, *Le Peintre*. The gems were from the American Museum of Natural History's unprecedented exhibition of famous gemstones, *The Nature Of Diamonds*, which was widely seen as one of the most comprehensive displays of precious stones ever mounted. Elizabeth Taylor's emerald-cut Krupp diamond, given to her by Richard Burton, may be one of the stones now lying at the bottom of the sea off Peggy's Cove, although neither Swissair nor the American Museum of Natural History are prepared to identify the owners.

This may seem shamelessly incidental but such is Taylor's mystique that there is endless speculation about almost anything pertaining to her. In November 1998 Patrizia Reggiani, known as the 'Black Widow', was found guilty of ordering the murder of fashion heir Maurizio Gucci and sentenced to twenty-nine years in prison. Gucci was shot dead, mafia-style, as he walked to his office in 1995. Before greed for Gucci's inheritance and an overwhelming desire to gain revenge for the acrimonious break-up of her marriage to Maurizio twisted her mind, the 50-year-old Reggiani was fêted by all of Italy's large-circulation newspapers as the Elizabeth Taylor of Milan's high society. Reggiani not only loved the Taylor association, she actively cultivated it, because it had less to do with her fatal gold-digging habits than her fabulously surreal lifestyle.

That Taylor's very name continues to be a yardstick by which glamour and excess are measured, is as much a compelling mystery as her supernatural sticking power. In an era obsessed with fleeting images of celebrity and 'the next big thing', Taylor is the ultimate campaigner. She is one of the original survivors of the biggest growth industry of the twentieth century: fame. One hundred years ago the average person would only have 'known' a handful of people that he or she hadn't met personally: the royal family, politicians and a few military and theatrical stars. Today all of us 'know' hundreds, perhaps thousands of people that we have never actually seen in the flesh. However, few stars in any walk of life have ever been as fêted, or courted fame with the same appetite, as Elizabeth Taylor.

One of the most celebrated society snappers in the world, Richard Young, tells how a photograph of Taylor made his career. He gatecrashed a party Liz was throwing for Richard Burton at the Dorchester and, before he was thrown out, managed to shoot a roll of the couple cutting the cake. He was paid £5,000 for the film, a huge amount in those days. 'That's when I gave up the day job,' says Young, who went on to join the paparazzi to hunt down screen icons such as Taylor because photographs of them were a licence to print money.

She will never recapture the almost nonchalant sexuality of her neurotic, frustrated Maggie in *Cat On A Hot Tin Roof*, or the wonderfully cheap charisma of her 1960 Oscar-winning, good-time girl in *Butterfield 8*, or even the voluptuous, sleepy boredom of her fly-blown Cleopatra, but the myth still flourishes.

Unlike Elvis Presley, whose excesses rapidly killed him, Taylor has survived numerous death scares, while seeming almost to thrive on her own extremes. In fact, Liz's first brush with death was on camera. Early on in her career, MGM lent their child star to Twentieth Century Fox for her fourth movie – *Jane Eyre* – the 1944 film

The cat reclines: Liz's performance in Tennessee Williams's sizzling screenplay, Cat On
A Hot Tin Roof, *bolstered her credentials as a serious Hollywood player*

starring Margaret O'Brien and Peggy Ann Garner, the hottest child stars at the time. Liz wasn't even mentioned in the credits. Prophetically, perhaps, in her one big scene in the film, she died of tuberculosis. Many of her closest friends are now dead: Roddy McDowall, Montgomery Clift, James Dean, Rock Hudson, Mike Todd and, of course, Richard Burton. And the longer she goes on, the more she reminds me of Shakespeare's Margaret of Anjou, the battling queen who somehow manages to survive several royal dynasties and an inordinately large chunk of the Bard's history plays. The extraordinary list of characters who galloped across Liz's stage is no less dashing and preposterous than Shakespeare's: Michael Jackson, Larry Fortensky, Eddie Fisher, Michael Wilding and countless others.

Whether Taylor still has a glittering acting career ahead of her is open to speculation. It will need a director with a magic touch; someone like Quentin Tarantino who has a rare gift for restoring careers that have slipped out of sight. Tarantino did it for John Travolta in *Pulp Fiction* and Pam Grier and Robert Forster in *Jackie Brown*. Taylor's fans live in hope. But I somehow doubt that such a movie will ever be made.

Chapter I

Hollywood Lolita

Elizabeth Taylor was, according to Hollywood legend, invented by the studios, namely the mighty MGM. If Hollywood's manipulation of female child stars has changed dramatically from Shirley Temple to Drew Barrymore, the turning point was the young English girl, born on 27 February 1932 at Heathwood, 8 Wildwood Road, London NW11.

Taylor's parents were American. Her father, Francis, hailed from Illinois and was a moderately successful art dealer who worked the art markets in Europe and shipped paintings over to New York for his uncle, Howard Young, to sell on to the great and good. Her mother, Sara Warnbrodt, was a minor theatrical star who, under the stage name Sara Sothern, enjoyed her finest hour on Broadway playing a crippled girl who is cured, in a sentimental melodrama called *The Fool* written by Channing Pollock. It was Sara who groomed her daughter for the showbusiness world when the family moved back to the States on the eve of World War II.

Having enjoyed a healthy, upper middle-class social profile in London, the Taylors were eager to create the same kind of opportunities for themselves in California, where Howard Young had opened another branch of his art business. In short, that meant mixing socially with the Hollywood aristocracy who ran the movie business. With Young's contacts in the art world, the doors duly started opening for the Taylors. Liz's mother was ambitious for her daughter in the stereotypical way mothers have of vicariously fulfilling their own ambitions through their offspring. Shirley Temple's mother is perhaps the most famous example of this,

14

We're all going on a summer holiday: the toddler Liz, aged two, getting to grips
with her first boat. Even at this tender age she had those magnetic eyes

A luminous Liz on the knee of her mother, Sara, flanked by her brother Howard

imploring her daughter to 'Sparkle, Shirley, sparkle' from the wings. The curly-topped starlet was the biggest box-office draw in the world by the age of seven. But despite the studio's efforts and her precocious magic in front of the camera, Shirley Temple's career fizzled out quite early and the film she made in her late teens – which saw her first screen kiss – was an almighty flop. Her fans simply could not make the imaginative leap between the singing and dancing tot to a sexually charged young woman on the verge of adulthood. Shirley retired at 22, and in one of the more peculiar quirks of acting fortunes was appointed US Ambassador to Ghana in 1974.

The nine-year-old Elizabeth, already startlingly beautiful, was destined to break the mould of cute Hollywood moppets. She first excited interest from Universal Studios, which signed her up in 1941. It was a short-lived affair that produced one inconsequential film, *One Born Every Minute*, directed by Harold Young (no relation) in 1942. Despite the somewhat cursory way in which Universal terminated the contract six months later, Sara Taylor was undeterred and managed to push her daughter onto the payroll of MGM, which was looking for an English girl to play opposite Roddy McDowall, another English evacuee, in *Lassie Come Home* (directed by Fred M Wilcox, 1943).

Although it wasn't an enormous part, Taylor made a deep impression on a generation of schoolchildren. This was one of the first Technicolor movies ever made and it has bewitched many successive generations, since. The perky scenes with the little girl in the wilds of Scotland, her head buried in Lassie's mane, have left an indelible impression on children around the world for more than fifty years.

With the benefit of hindsight, what was outstanding about this most maudlin of matinées could be written on the back of a lollipop wrapper. What was remarkable, at least from Hollywood's point of view – although it was one shared by her co-star, Roddy McDowall, who played Lassie's rightful young owner – was the young Taylor's assurance in front of the camera. McDowall, already an established star following his performance in the 1941 Oscar-winning film, *How Green Was My Valley*, was an important ally in Taylor's early career. Like Liz, he was one of the few child prodigies who made the leap to become an adult star. He would remain one of the very few friends on whom she could rely.

Despite being dubbed the new male Shirley Temple, Roddy McDowall was astute enough to avoid that awful fate. He made engaging appearances in a string of 1940s hit films, but as he grew older, he quickly tired of being typecast by directors who insisted on still seeing him as an English adolescent. In the early 1950s he

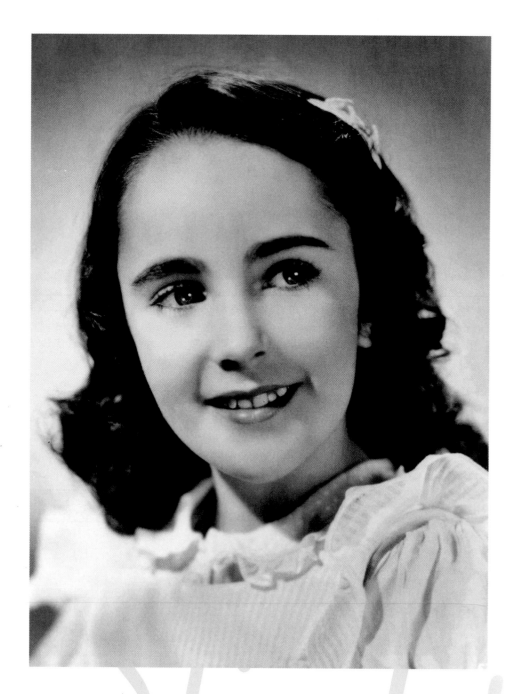

Portrait of a child: the contrast between her dark features and translucent skin gifted Liz an eerie beauty

abandoned Hollywood for New York and emerged just ten years later as a versatile and dedicated character actor, still in the the bloom of youth. McDowall finally found the fame he craved as Galen, the cerebral monkey in the *Planet Of The Apes* film series. He was reunited with Taylor in 1963 in *Cleopatra*, by which time her fame wildly eclipsed his own.

For the young, luminously beautiful Liz, a flurry of small roles in sentimental weepies followed *Lassie Come Home* until *National Velvet* in 1944. This is the film that made her the Macaulay Culkin of her generation. Directed by Clarence Brown, and co-starring Mickey Rooney as the ex-jockey who nurses Velvet Brown's pubescent dream to whip her sorrel gelding over Aintree's famous jumps and win the Grand National, the film was an instant and massive success.

Set in a tiny Sussex village, *National Velvet* tells the story of horse-mad Velvet, who wins a horse in a raffle. She asks Rooney to help her train the animal to run in the Grand National, but the entrance fee is too high for her family to afford. Anne Revere, who won Best Supporting Actress Oscar for the role of Liz's mother, then stumps up the money she had won years before as the prize for swimming the English Channel. In one of the best horse-racing sequences ever filmed – the editing of which won Robert J Kern an Oscar – Taylor wins the National, only to be disqualified for being a girl. It took another thirty-three years for the powers that be at Aintree to allow female jockeys to contest the race. But Liz's performance sowed the seeds. Originally the producer, Pandro S Berman, thought Taylor too frail for the role. Her mother promptly put her on such a severe training programme of eating and swimming that she not only grew several inches, but dramatically filled out to look older than her years.

It was the point of no turning back in Taylor's career. MGM and Louis B Mayer sank their corporate teeth into their 'rapturously beautiful' (critic James Agee) new star and started taking over every corner of her life. As Alexander Walker points out in his seminal biography, *Elizabeth*, Taylor 'gained nearly all her education from the age of 12 on the MGM studio lot in the privileged but isolated building now known as The Little Red Schoolhouse'. Her classmates were other child stars and, as far as the rest of the world was concerned, her well-publicized love affair with animals supplanted the role of boyfriends.

This sweeter-than-thou image couldn't last for long. The teenage Elizabeth may have had the face of a child, but her eyes and shapely body belied her tender years. She was breathtakingly beautiful and indolently sexy. Looking back at early stills from her movies, or flicking through her first promotional photographs, it's striking

Puppy love: Liz's first infatuation was with animals

how much of a contradiction Liz was in physical terms. The person who stares back at you from these images is still a child, but the eyes look wise and knowing. As her figure rapidly filled out, the sexual charisma became as impossible to ignore as it was to disguise. She was the very stuff of infatuation. Her presence in the stifling conditions of the MGM studios must have excited as much comment then as talk of Lolitas does today.

MGM took a gamble in daring to promote her public image in a way that had never been done before. Elizabeth was deliberately marketed in a manner that close rivals, such as Judy Garland or Shirley Temple, never could be marketed, namely with raw sexual allure. Garland, Taylor's elder by ten years, was never more successful in her short, tragic life than as a teenage star, becoming a legend at 17 as Dorothy in Victor Fleming's *Wizard Of Oz* (1939). Despite the efforts of her husband Vincente Minnelli, who cast her in four of her best and most touching adult films, *Meet Me In St*

Louis (1944), *The Clock* (1945), *Ziegfeld Follies* (1946) and *The Pirate* (1948), Judy was never destined to be the heartbreaker that Liz was to become.

As Alexander Walker notes: 'Between her fourteenth and fifteenth birthdays, she [Taylor] developed the bust and some of the other physical attributes of a ripening girl in her late teens or early twenties. Before she was even sixteen, she was displaying a thirty-five inch bosom, thirty-four inch hips and a twenty-two inch waist, which she used to pinch even more tightly into the dirndl peasant skirts then fashionable.' When Orson Welles first saw Liz in the flesh, probably on the set of *Jane Eyre*, in which he starred, and in which she played a waif dying of cruel negligence, he too was stunned by the Lolita-like aura that Liz generated so effortlessly.

It must have been something of a retrospective fantasy on Welles' part, considering that Nabokov's story of the infatuation of the middle-aged lecher, Humbert Humbert, with a sexually forward child of 12 wasn't written until 1955 when Liz was 22 years old.

Welles' sentiment, however, was not misplaced. An apocryphal story circulates about how the teenage Taylor excited comments about 'jail bait' from the studio lackeys, who used to watch her eat in the canteen. Considering that Liz was so far removed from the acned trials and tribulations of ordinary college girls of her own age, she probably had no idea what effect her burgeoning sexuality had on people. In those days 'dates' were organized by the studios and her mother to give the press something to write about. By all accounts these were tepid, almost scripted non-events. One can imagine a queue of hot-housed young male wannabe stars escorting Liz to preppy tea parties. But it's unlikely that MGM would ever allow any of them to compromise, let alone kiss, their star product. It must have been intensely frustrating for the adolescent Liz to find herself on the end of a leash held not by an overprotective parent, but a studio marketing machine.

It was a decisive feature in Liz's budding career. Here was an adolescent who clearly wasn't allowed to make her own choices and therefore the mistakes from which she could learn. She was never allowed to mature 'naturally', with all the haphazard pain and joy that that entails. To do so might well embarrass the men who had invested so much time and money in their fledgling film star. Teenagers who are allowed to indulge their whims, or give vent to their natural, hormone-driven impulses, frequently embarrass those charged with the guardianship of their well-being. Parents of 'normal' teenagers may accept that their teen offspring may well cause them some trouble since it's a part of growing up (they themselves probably did the same to their parents). Liz, though, was neither 'normal', nor in the charge of her natural parents. She was a very precious commodity, an asset that had to be protected and nurtured so that it could return the dividends they expected. In effect, Liz was denied some of the most basic and essential lessons of growing up. The long-term repercussions would have enormous impact on her future behaviour.

Ironically, it was Judy Garland's husband, Vincente Minnelli, who helped usher in Liz's celluloid 'maturity' in *Father Of The Bride* (1950) and the less effective sequel, *Father's Little Dividend* (1951). The first film is a thoroughly enchanting domestic comedy about the trials and tribulations facing a middle-aged family man, played by Spencer Tracy, when his daughter, Kay (Taylor), decides that she wants to get married. Riddled with bleak undercurrents of jealousy, insecurity and fears about growing old, Tracy is superbly neurotic in the role. Inflated with pride at the sight of his beautiful daughter and her imminent marriage, but crumpled by the fact that she loves someone else (Don Taylor), Tracy's Stanley T Banks stews in juices that, were it not for his self-deprecating comic brilliance, would be almost incestuous.

Charles Shyer's 1991 remake with Steve Martin, Diane Keaton and Kimberley Williams has none of the tenderness and spicy chemistry of the original. Elizabeth is wonderfully winsome. Joan Bennett (Liz's mum) is hysterically pragmatic. And Tracy is just fabulously disgruntled. Throughout the late 1940s and early 1950s, Liz played a stack of those poor little rich girls. Sweet without being sticky, possessed with grown-up eyes, Liz's teenage femmes were preppy characters who exuded an unsettling sexuality. Her voice, high-pitched and breathy (as it has always remained), coupled with the remnants of an English accent, added a sheen of mystique and dignity.

This is not to say that there weren't some appalling films made by MGM which starred Taylor during this period. Sheridan Morley astutely notes in his excellent biography, *Elizabeth Taylor* (Pavilion Books, reprinted 1998), that unlike her contemporaries, who desperately wanted to be discovered, the young Liz was blessed and cursed by her total lack of ambition. She didn't come up the hard way through a life of deprivation and family disasters. Totally protected by her mother and the studio, Liz simply glided from movie to movie. Because it was the only kind of life that she had ever known, it didn't even occur to her to wonder whether she could do it or not. She was therefore spared the agony of insecurity and (unfortunately, in a lot of instances) script choice. Frothy teenage romances such as *A Date With Judy* (directed by Richard Thorpe, 1948) and *Julia Misbehaves* (directed by Jack Conway, 1948), were followed by misconceived monstrosities such as

Liz and Howard in England during their school years in Hampstead

At home with her dolls: the twelve-year-old Liz stitches clothes for playmates

Victor Saville's disastrous melodrama, *Conspirator* (1949), and Norman Krasna's witless romantic comedy, complete with talking dog, *The Big Hangover* (1950). Even MGM had doubts about the wisdom of releasing *Conspirator*, co-starring 38-year-old Robert Taylor as Liz's romantic interest. They held on to it for over a year, hoping against hope that its patriotic finale would overcome its general ghastliness. The answer, concluded *The New York Times*, was a definite 'No'.

It was hardly surprising that Liz wanted an escape route out of this cul-de-sac, and fast. She must have been bored to the point of tears at times, even though from 1948 she was pocketing a cool $1,000 a week – more pay than any other contracted artiste of her generation. Liz longed for some sense of normality, yet she had no idea what that really meant. As a girl mostly reared on a diet of tediously conventional films and protected under the wing of her mother and her minders at MGM, the most obvious answer to the problem that presented itself was to get married. It was also, of course, a recipe for disaster. Liz isn't the first and certainly won't be the last

Hollywood star to use this particular parachute to bail out of the business. She was simply one of the most unlucky ones.

But Liz was never destined to escape her fame through her marriages. Nothing makes a studio more nervous than a star product with an itchy wedding finger or even worse, a desire to become pregnant. Finding a fiancé was never going to be a problem. Placating the understandably furious studio bosses was another matter entirely. First over the edge was a squeaky-clean army football star, Glenn Davis, who met the sixteen-and-a-half-year-old Liz at a Malibu party. To the delight of the gossips, there were soon rumours of engagement in the air. By the time Liz had finished *The Conspirator* some six months later, and become briefly infatuated with her co-star Peter Lawford, Davis was already a football statistic. Next up was William D Pawley, the wealthy son of a former American Ambassador to Brazil. At 28 he was a clear decade older than Liz, but much more sophisticated than Davis, and promised a life no less lucrative than the career she was expected to give up. Liz duly collected her second diamond ring, one of at least a dozen that she would pick up over the next thirty years. What crushed this budding relationship was a film that changed Liz's profile forever.

Seeking to mint more money from their young but now engaged star, MGM lent Liz out to Paramount Studios for a classic production that not only established her own raven-haired beauty, but also set a popular standard for a decade. It was the first truly startling transformation for Liz, from cute bobby sox lass to *femme fatale*, and it mapped out a whole new, unexplored and massive box-office potential. The potential was sex; the film was *A Place In The Sun* (1951), a directorial masterpiece by George Stevens and essential viewing for all Liz fans. Pawley's interest in Liz duly wilted under the glare of the ensuing publicity. He was no longer dating a conventional teenage star; he was dating a blossoming sex symbol. The film opens with Montgomery Clift's beach bum, George Eastman, trying to hitch a lift to an unnamed town. A beautiful brunette in a sports car whizzes by, toots her horn and disappears, only for Clift to rediscover that she's his rich cousin and the daughter of the boss who puts him to work in a factory.

Based on a true story and the classic novel by Theodore Dreiser, *An American Tragedy*, the film takes a searing look at Clift's social-climbing nobody, who may or may not have murdered his pregnant girlfriend so that he can join the jet set. Hungry for love, eager to be accepted and doomed to fail, Clift and Taylor turned the American Dream into the sourest of American tragedies. Shot with unflinching close-ups of Clift and Taylor in passionate embraces, it not only raised eyebrows but also lifted six Oscars, thanks to indelible performances from Clift, Shelley Winters as the jilted working-class girlfriend and Taylor as the West Coast's sexiest debutante. As David Thomson writes in his *Biographical Dictionary Of Film*: 'In the forty years since, has any movie actress been so blatant about extraordinary beauty? These days, few people can carry such looks without irony or a blush.' Thomson's comments raise two issues that Hollywood has been wrestling with uneasily ever since cameras started to roll: sex and the teenage starlet; and the warping effects of sudden massive fame on child actors.

Liz once famously grumbled: 'How can I concentrate on my education when Robert Taylor keeps sticking his tongue down my throat?' After *A Place In The Sun*, Liz's box-office appeal, already high, simply soared. With it came some unsavoury attentions. Howard Hughes, the US tycoon – who was already middle-aged and something of a recluse – saw a photo-spread of Liz in *Life* magazine, became infatuated and arranged meetings where he sweet-talked her parents, and tried literally to buy his way into her affections. Having made the classic film, *Hell's Angels* (1930), about aviators in World War I, and scored successes with *Scarface* (1932) and *The Outlaw* (1943), Hughes was no stranger to the film world or film stars. He was used to getting his own way. It was he who coined the phrase 'platinum blonde' and he dated some of the most desirable movie stars of the era, including Jean Harlow and Katharine Hepburn. If Liz's young flesh mesmerized him, then her home-grown reserve must have bamboozled him.

It's impossible to gauge how deeply this attention must have affected the emotionally adolescent Liz. She had no real friends of her own age and in comparable situations. The main danger for her at this time was that, rather than offering a leg up the celluloid ladder, such success could spell the kiss of death. In a way, *A Place In The Sun* was the Becher's Brook of her career. Like every famous starlet then and ever since, Liz cleared this famous National fence without knowing where she might land or how much further she could go. During the filming of *A Place In The Sun* in 1951, the director, George Stevens, ordered the bathing suit-clad Liz to run into the freezing waters of Lake Tahoe for take after take. Watching on the sidelines, her mother complained bitterly that her daughter was having her period and that exposure to cold water might harm her. Liz called in sick for the next three days, and, for the next twenty years, she reputedly refused to work during her monthly cycles. One wonders whether Liz might have been tempted to pull the plug on her career at this early stage. She may not have had to stretch to the sexual indignities of subsequent teen stars, but she was no less susceptible to the humiliation and furore

Liz in National Velvet *uniform. She grew several inches in a matter of months on a high protein diet and plenty of swimming to secure the role*

Tuppence a bag: Liz sweet-talking an exotic bird

The all-American look: all prepped up and nowhere to go

Liz in the famous Little Red Schoolhouse, the classroom on the MGM lot where the young stars went to school

her films sometimes generated in her career and private life. The crucial difference is that Liz endured and at times even thrived on the adversity. To give some small measure of that achievement, we need only look at the testimony of some of the starlets who have followed in Liz's wake.

Sue Lyon, the lollipop-sucking star in Stanley Kubrick's 1962 film of *Lolita*, now in her fifties, says: 'I defy any girl rocketed to fame at 15 in a sex-nymphet role to stay on an even keel.' After appearing in John Huston's *The Night Of The Iguana* (1964) – ironically opposite Richard Burton when he was still married to Taylor – Sue Lyon slipped into obscurity via drug addiction and a series of misguided marriages, including one to a convicted murderer. Brooke Shields, dubbed the most beautiful woman in the world aged 11, when she was served up as a prostitute in Louis Malle's *Pretty Baby* (1978), has had a haphazard film career ever since, though her 1990s television role in the American sitcom *Suddenly Susan* is a popular success. Linda Blair was only 14 when she was called upon to rape herself with a crucifix in *The Exorcist* (1973). After the furore over the film died down, Blair slumped into a hellish, sex-and-drugs binge that ended up with her being wanted by the FBI for cocaine peddling. She turned up again in *Exorcist II* (1977), but her credibility (despite more than thirty movies) has shrivelled and she is reduced to quirky cameos.

Maria Schneider sums it up for most of those who are branded with an iconic tag in their teens. An alluring vixen herself in 1973 when she starred, aged 19, with Marlon Brando in *Last Tango In Paris*, she is now a world-weary lesson to newcomers. Maria is convinced, despite seeing the funereal face of Jeremy Irons in orgasmic embrace with 14-year-old Dominique Swain in the controversial remake of *Lolita*, that nothing in Hollywood has changed to make teenage girls anything but the victims of male dominance and ambition. 'I had no idea,' she says in a recent *Sunday Times* interview with Garth Pearce, 'what I was letting myself in for.' Her career has never recovered from the ensuing outrage. Like Taylor, Schneider says 'I was no more than a baby at 19. I was a virgin. Yet it seems to me that nothing has been learnt by Hollywood or agents who set up these deals. They keep putting older men with very young women. Never the other way around.'

These pressures placed on a teenage Liz had very different consequences. The wheels tumbled off her marriages, and sometimes her sanity, and latterly her all-important career. But almost perversely, all this adversity only enhanced her appeal. Apart from Liz, perhaps only Jodie Foster can claim to be a stayer after she played the child prostitute Iris in Martin Scorsese's *Taxi Driver* (1976) at the age of 13. Curiously, her deadpan performance and her unconscious ignorance of the film's shock value exactly mirror Liz's own apparent naivety of her screen allure. Foster has had her own battles to fight, but she also had Liz's experience to refer to. In the 1950s family values still had the upper hand and journalists were more restrained in their reporting. Although the studios still called the shots, Elizabeth Taylor was about to change all that. And how.

A sign of things to come: Liz shows a daring flash of tummy while modelling a blue check pant suit

The most glamorous beachcomber on the West Coast

CHAPTER II

IMPULSIVE BRIDE/SERIAL ADULTERESS

ecause she had been married eight times to seven different men, Elizabeth Taylor's love-life soon became of far greater interest to the public than any screen role she ever played. The Henry VIII of her generation, she did not actually behead any of her spouses after they had fallen from favour but she certainly cut most of them down to size. For Liz, Mr Right was forever turning into Mr Wrong. For better or worse, high-profile divorce proceedings became Liz's trademark. Since 1950, she made divorce not just the preserve of the glamorous rich, but a routine hazard for a generation of frustrated housewives. The irony might be lost on Liz, but in Japan today there is a self-help magazine on divorce and how to get it which is named after her. It's hardly Liz's most salubrious claim to fame in the East, but in a society as tightly regulated as Japan's, it's no mean indication of the kind of effect her own marriages have had on our perception of the institution.

With the benefit of hindsight, why on Earth did Liz Taylor bother? The simple answer is that the young Elizabeth genuinely bought into the whole romantic live-happily-ever-after myth of marriage so enthusiastically endorsed by Hollywood films. For mere mortals, who suffer a string of marital failures, the obvious logic is to forget the rings and expensive morning suits and wallow in sin. But Liz was, and remains, a preposterously optimistic romantic and, despite the haystack of husbands, also strangely conventional. After her seventh marriage, she still protested: 'I have to be in love to sleep with a man. And when I am really in love, I want to be married.'

One of the most desirable women in the world...

Taylor

...in one of the most unflattering costumes ever made

She was also, in the late 1940s and early 1950s, blind to the fact that the unreal pampered life of a star is not conducive to the compromises and patience required to keep a marriage on the rails. Liz longed for a husband whom she could admire and who would control her. She was not easily tamed. Liz had and still possesses a wit as sharp as a switchblade, and few men – really only Mike Todd among her first four wedding breakfasts – was her temperamental equal.

Liz was by no means the only star to have indulged in serial marriages. Lana Turner, Mickey Rooney, Stan Laurel and Zsa Zsa Gabor all married eight times. But Liz's various marriages actually had the bizarre effect of increasing rather than diluting her allure. The tabloids loved her for it. Whether they were slating or deifying her, she provided them with a soap opera that never looked as though it would run out of steam.

For the young Liz, a husband was almost a mystical necessity. More often than not, Liz put men on pedestals and time and time again they obligingly, predictably and even comically fell off. Liz longed for the fairy-tale union. She frequently protested to the press that she would be entirely happy to give up her career to become a good wife and mother. Every half-baked analyst claimed that what she desperately needed was to love and be loved. That, and the fact that she could not stand being alone.

It was true. Since her childhood Liz had always been praised and pampered. Why shouldn't a husband continue this trend? She didn't get off to the greatest start. At the age of 17, with two broken engagements behind her and probably rocked by the strength of the negative publicity of being dubbed 'Liz the Jilt', she was determined to get it right. The man she fell in love with at a cocktail party, Nicky Hilton, heir to the Hilton Hotel fortune, was outwardly perfect marriage material. Fabulously wealthy, good-looking and able to flatter a young star with his lavish lifestyle, Nicky was God's gift to a Hollywood princess. On paper, Disney couldn't have scripted a more perfect partner for her.

For the gossips, it was a fairy-tale match of business wealth and Hollywood glamour, and MGM financed the wedding in the manner of an indulgent parent, quite unlike Spencer Tracy's character in *Father Of The Bride*. On 6 May 1950, the day of the wedding in Beverly Hills, Liz herself looked starry-eyed. The sensual and breathtaking beauty that captivated her audiences was on full display for the assembled paparazzi and eager onlookers. During the engagement, Liz had wowed the cameras with her revealing necklines and lingering kisses with Nicky. When she kissed him at the altar, the kiss went on so long that the priest reportedly had to intervene and break up the moment of passion. Although numerous rumours about Nicky Hilton's prolific gambling, drinking, womanizing and violent temper had surfaced over the preceding weeks, Liz was perhaps too naive and lovestruck to take much notice. She later recalled how she was totally unprepared for the shock of the honeymoon. Hilton's attention and charm apparently vanished overnight and Liz found herself married to a crass, chauvinistic, spoilt child, with whom she had nothing in common apart from a shared address.

Liz famously commented that the marriage lasted two weeks… the honeymoon managed somewhat longer. On their three-month cruise through Europe, Hilton spent his most meaningful hours in the casinos. Liz, being under-age, wasn't allowed to enter. For Hilton, marrying, or perhaps acquiring, Liz was a gargantuan ego-trip, a luxury purchase as empty of meaning as one of his vastly over-priced hotels. Hilton was Mr Playboy; to all intents and purposes, she was Playmate of the Month. Nicky had racy tastes and his appetite for drink and women can hardly have made him the most stable of partners and escorts.

Liz arrived home from ther jaunt some 20 pounds lighter, with bruises up her arms, chain-smoking and nurturing an ulcer. She was desperately unhappy and alone. At first she couldn't admit to the world that the fairy-tale marriage had quickly become a sham, possibly because the shame was too great, and she also feared the effect that negative publicity might have on a career which now ironically looked like being her main chance of escape from a domestic hell. Nicky Hilton had no such qualms about submitting his quarrels for press scrutiny. For him, being married to a Hollywood institution cramped his style and ultimately proved as liberating as a ball and chain.

In December poor Liz had to make the decision that had been staring her in the face since the second week of her honeymoon. She filed for divorce, citing extreme mental cruelty. During her short-lived first marriage, she fainted on the set of *Father's Little Dividend* and later miscarried. This was probably fortuitous, given Nicky's alleged wife-beating and inclinations towards abusive behaviour. According to Kitty Kelley, controversial author of *Elizabeth Taylor: The Last Star* (Michael Joseph, 1981), this was the beginning of a pattern that Liz would follow for the rest of her life. When the stresses and strains of a roller-coaster personal and professional life became too much, she would go into hospital. Nicky Hilton himself would have two more failed marriages before he died of his own excesses aged 42. The following January, Liz would collapse with a viral infection and nervous exhaustion. It can hardly have helped that the film with which the studio celebrated her return to the fold was

Elizabeth was ever the sensational bride

Number One: Liz and her first husband Nicky Hilton tied the knot in May 1950 in Beverly Hills.
Despite the ritzy send off, the couple would separate within six months, and divorce the following year

called *Love Is Better Than Ever*. Though the film was an out-and-out flop, Liz's recovery was considerably helped by the romantic attentions of the director, Stanley Donen, a hugely talented 27-year-old choreographer who had made significant splashes as a director of both *On The Town* and *Singin' In The Rain*. Their burgeoning romance was serious enough to worry MGM, and the studio sent Liz to England to film *Ivanhoe* in order to get her away from Donen. In the studio's eyes, divorce was one thing, but to be openly courting so soon afterwards was another thing entirely. Hollywood was scandalized when the 19-year-old divorcee Liz was cited as 'the other woman' in Stanley Donen's divorce.

MGM's policy worked in some respects. Richard Thorpe's vintage epic unscrupulously and inaccurately ransacked Sir Walter Scott's classic adventure tale. But it was an enjoyable romp for Liz – nothing less than a breath of fresh air. Stanley Donen was duly forgotten, but Liz rapidly fell under the spell of another actor, Michael Wilding. Wilding was the antithesis of Nicky Hilton. Twenty years older than Liz, the well-known British actor was the epitome of the English gentleman. The son of a career army officer and an actress, Wilding was polished, charming and the leading man of the British screen. He started out as a portrait painter and commercial artist, and in 1933 joined the art department of a British film studio. Wilding soon switched to acting on the London stage, graduated to film and by the late 1940s had become a popular star, specializing in patrician roles. It's undoubtedly this facet of his character and career that seduced Liz.

Cultured, gentle and reserved, Wilding represented for Liz the kind of security and maturity that she must have felt she needed in herself. All of the things anyone could possibly want and desire, in fact, in a matinée idol father-figure. Though attracted to Liz, Michael Wilding did not initially pursue the dewy-eyed star. He was, though separated, still married to Kay Young. And he probably felt, unlike a host of drooling middle-aged would-be suitors, that Liz was too young.

Typically, Liz was not to be deterred. Once she set her mind on something, she could be as tenacious and thick-skinned as her mother. After the delinquent behaviour of Nicky Hilton, Liz saw in Wilding an ideal husband and, more importantly, a good father to the children she desperately wanted to have. It was she who bought the ring and apparently popped the big question. You don't need the vantage point of retrospect to realize this marriage of complete opposites was doomed to be a lopsided affair. Wilding was a carbon copy hero from a Jane Austen novel: a Mr Knightly to a young and wilful Emma. So it would prove with Liz and Michael. The gossip columns talked up the age gap and Liz's need for a father figure.

It was true, but the simple fact of the matter was that Michael Wilding would prove too gentle and old-fashioned to stand up to an ego that had been polished since childhood by the tireless press.

Liz moved her new husband back to Los Angeles, a move that was to prove disastrous for Wilding's career. He stuck out like a sore thumb in Tinseltown. He was too English and too unambitious for a cutthroat environment like Hollywood, and his understated English charm was lost on the studios like so many cuttings. The couple were also amazingly broke and the story goes that, due to currency restrictions, Wilding left England with virtually nothing. In fact, he had to pay off an enormous tax bill before he was allowed to leave.

Liz, who had done little acting while shopping around for her new husband, was forced back into the harness with MGM, despite becoming pregnant soon after the marriage. It was a Faustian pact in the making. Liz's career was not flourishing. She lost several good films to up-and-coming actresses. *Young Bess* went to Jean Simmons and *Roman Holiday* was awarded to Audrey Hepburn. Blonde competition was also looming in the shapely figures of Grace Kelly and Marilyn Monroe, and Liz found herself unceremoniously toppled from her position as Hollywood's number one star. Unlike Kelly and Monroe, however, Liz never lost that sense of being Hollywood family. In this she was unique or, if not unique, certainly the last true survivor of Hollywood's old-style dynasties.

Despite have been temporarily out of favour, MGM's favourite prodigal daughter still managed to negotiate contracts for both herself and her new husband. She received $5,000 a week for five years, while Wilding earned $3,000 a week for three years, with forty weeks a year guaranteed. The studio also granted the Wildings $50,000 to buy a house. However, the price Liz had to pay for all this good fortune was a series of dreadfully poor scripts. Despite her continuing pregnancy, Liz took on *The Girl Who Had Everything* while she could still work. Top billing did nothing to prevent it being an out-and-out flop, with weird camera angles having to be used to disguise her bulge.

The arrival of Michael Howard Wilding Junior, on 6 January 1953, delighted Liz and chilled the blood of the studios, who promptly stopped her salary until she got back into shape. However idyllic, a great family life could not disguise impending financial catastrophe for the Wildings. Wilding Senior's career had stalled in Hollywood. He was disillusioned with California and was constantly being miscast in small, ridiculous parts. And he leaned heavily on Taylor's kudos for professional favours. He was also growing spectacularly lazy and refused to appear in *Latin Lover*

The dashing Nicky Hilton and Liz enjoying one of their rare moments of harmony

Mr and Mrs Michael Wilding at the premiere of Ivanhoe at the Empire Cinema in Leicester Square. Unknown to the world, Liz was already pregnant with her first child

almost certainly because he felt it was beneath his dignity – and so he was duly suspended by the studio. Michael Wilding couldn't care less. Naturally indolent, he much preferred lounging around at home and enjoyed the Hollywood social life, where his easy charm made him widely acceptable to the other loafers in the film colony. But his lack of ambition did not endear him to an increasingly grumpy Liz who, as a new mother, was understandably reluctant to take on the role of breadwinner as well as mother.

Amazingly, Liz's career could have been well and truly over at this juncture if it hadn't been for Vivien Leigh, or at least Vivien Leigh's sundry misfortunes. During the filming of *Elephant Walk*, Leigh suffered the biggest in a series of nervous breakdowns, which would eventually ruin her career and – ultimately – cause her to take her life. Paramount, the producers, were desperate for a replacement and Liz, despite being twenty years younger, fitted the bill. The sultry story of an illicit romance with Peter Finch in a cholera-infested tea plantation won few plaudits but it prompted the neurotic MGM to put Liz back on the payroll. This despite some serious health problems. While doing publicity stills for *Elephant Walk* in May 1953, Liz experienced the first of a truly freakish series of accidents. She was sitting in a jeep with Peter Finch and Dana Andrews, posing for publicity stills, when a rusty splinter from the wind machine was blown into her eye. Consequently, an ulcer developed and Liz had to have surgery to save her sight.

The incident could, again, have killed her career. But battling Liz recovered and MGM duly cast her as a frigid English matron in yet another flop, *The Girl Who Had Everything*. The studio didn't seem to know what to do with Liz, or how to cast her. She was in something of a limbo, still looking for the part that would underline all that beauty and potential. But at least they were paying while she more or less sleepwalked through various hoops. The awful *Rhapsody*, with Vittorio Gassman, was rapidly followed by *Beau Brummel*, another English costume drama capitalizing on the success of *Ivanhoe*.

Sheridan Morley notes in his biography of Liz that 'The film achieved a kind of immortality by becoming the least suitable ever to have been set before the Queen at a Royal Film Performance.' This was specifically because it featured Sheridan's father, Robert Morley, as one of the Queen's mad ancestors, George III, who tries to strangle the future George IV (Peter Ustinov). The critics had a field day.

Meanwhile, the Wilding marriage was falling apart at breakneck speed. As Liz was rediscovering her appetite for acting in the much-neglected film, *The Last Time I Saw Paris*, she began to view Michael not only as a real brake on her career, but as something of a bore. In the five years during which she had slummed through some of the most sludgy celluloid ever produced by a studio, and delivered Michael a second son (Christopher) on 27 February 1955, she had changed from a clinging child to an imperious young mother. Years later, Liz claimed that she could hardly remember the marriage at all.

Though still attached to Elizabeth, Wilding, for his part, found his wife's lack of domesticity infuriating. She was extremely untidy, could not boil an egg and kept a large number of animals in the home without bothering to clean up after them. The latter was to became a habit of a lifetime. In his diaries, Richard Burton notes that it was a daily routine to clean atrophied dog mess from the carpets. The undisgusted manner in which he put it suggests this came with the job of being married to Elizabeth.

By the time Christopher was born (by Caesarean section), Michael's role had receded to little more than that of Mr Elizabeth Taylor – an insecure slave to his wife's increasingly hostile moods. Professionally, he was considered a has-been, even as Liz, against a fair number of odds, was beginning to reassert her position as top star. Although it can by no means be described as a great film, *The Last Time I Saw Paris* had a profound effect on Liz. As she told one journalist, it was the first film that convinced her that she wanted to be an actress instead of just yawning her way through parts. Up to now, there had been a great deal to yawn through – including, it transpires, her role in her marriage.

The turning point was George Stevens' 1956 epic, *Giant*. Still unsure of how to exploit Liz, MGM lent her out to Warner Brothers. Instinctively aware that any film her old *A Place In The Sun* mentor worked on was not to be taken lightly, Liz determinedly lost a great deal of weight – perhaps too much – to star opposite Rock Hudson and James Dean. During the filming she suffered the first of many major intestinal problems and stalled completion of the film for two weeks. Back on the set in the Texas wasteland, however, she enjoyed hanging out with the boys, disappearing for intimate conversations with James Dean, and getting drunk on chocolate Martinis with Rock Hudson. Everything about the film is immense, towering and vast, including the egos that Stevens assembled. Liz and Hudson exceed themselves in demanding roles.

In Dean's case, it was a matter of a naturally great talent expanding in a part that gave him more freedom from the typecast role of young rebel. Lasting three hours and twenty minutes, this is no mere frolic. Rock plays an old-style J R Ewing (the *Dallas* anti-hero) cattle baron, who sweeps Liz off her feet and Dean is a chippy,

A night on the tiles: Liz, sporting a new haircut, and Michael Wilding have an evening on the town

An armful of trouble: the proud mother with Christopher and Michael Wilding Junior on her lap

Digger Barnes-like character, who discovers oil on land left to him by Hudson's sister. Liz is caught in the middle. It's a sprawling soap opera with an epic feel for the way the old sureties are gradually eroded by the new.

Liz became intimate friends with her two co-stars. Contrary to press rumours, it's unlikely that romance was involved. Rock Hudson's new wife, Nancy Gates, thought that he and Liz were having an affair. She was obviously not as clued-up about Hudson's homosexual inclinations as the gossip columnists. James Dean was someone that Liz could easily sink her teeth into. He was young, incredibly handsome, and at the time just as much of an icon as Liz. But it's unlikely that she ever did. Within a few weeks of the film's completion, James Dean died at the wheel of his Porsche when it lost control and threw him off the road. Liz retreated to hospital with a twisted colon, nervous depression and her marriage in free-fall.

Giant, however, was a $7-million money-spinner, the biggest film of the year and a decisive turning point in Taylor's career, not only because it won her her first Oscar nomination. Liz was still only 23 and once again, after *Giant*, she was fabulously bankable. The film of Edna Ferber's novel has been criticized for its sprawling attempts to launch some sort of attack on rampant materialism and many couldn't handle its plodding pace. It did, however, earn another Oscar nomination for Rock Hudson, who went on to be voted Hollywood's top box-office draw.

MGM, keen to cash in on the vogue for epics and galvanized by the success of Warner's film, brought Liz back into its plans and sank an unprecedented $6 million into Edward Dmytryk's 1957 movie, *Raintree County*. Liz, meanwhile, was once more blazing a trail through the tabloids with a series of rumoured affairs that included speculative liaisons with the likes of Victor Mature, Frank Sinatra and an Irish screenwriter, Keven McClory.

None of these supposed affairs came close to the drama surrounding the shooting of *Raintree County*. This Civil War extravaganza, billed by MGM as a successor to *Gone With The Wind*, was handsomely mounted and boasted a superb cast. However, it was dogged by problems and a story that didn't end at Appomattox, but ground on relentlessly until Liz's heroine could regain her Southern Belle sanity. Playing a spoilt lady from Southern aristocracy, Liz seduces and marries Montgomery Clift's anti-slavery student. Clift ditches his long-suffering girlfriend, marries Liz, becomes a schoolteacher and then goes off to fight on the side of the Unionists in the Civil War. Taylor's character's disturbing childhood comes back to haunt her. She goes insane and, with their young son, takes off in a storm in search of the legendary raintree.

The film is a lavish example of Hollywood indulgence. Despite expensive battle scenes, a grand ball sequence and reconstructed vintage towns and villages, it doesn't have the epic sweep and grandeur of *Gone With The Wind*. It also lacks a Clark Gable hero to sweep it – or its leading lady – off their feet. Much of the production cost was due to MGM's archaic way of throwing money about. A fortune was spent on Taylor's wardrobe, which was not only made up of the finest cloth for the outerwear, but also included expensive petticoats that were never seen. The studio still maintained the practice of full costuming for colour tests when, by the time of this film, colour was refined to the point of capturing exactly what was worn. On the sets, technicians turned up with equipment used in the silent era and some cameras were not even equipped for sound. Director Dmytryk had to remind some of his top technicians that technical improvements had been made since 1929. Needless to say, he alienated most of the crew.

Among the problems, the most expensive single mess was Montgomery Clift. During production, Clift, suffering from a colossal hangover and no sleep, drove into a telephone pole on his way back from a raucous night at Taylor's. The pole demolished the car and just missed his head. Liz arrived at the scene minutes later and saved the actor's life by pulling his teeth out of his throat. It was an amazingly cool-headed, selfless act by Liz, which nine out of ten people in the same position couldn't (or wouldn't) do. Officially, Clift suffered a broken nose, a gashed lip and his jaw was fractured in three places. In an equally unprecedented act of loyalty, Liz refused to go ahead with the production until Clift had recuperated. Without Liz, there was no film and so the studio duly bowed to her request.

Eight weeks later, filming recommenced. Surprisingly, Clift's physical damage is barely discernible on screen but a child could see that he looks a good ten years older, infinitely more gaunt and a lot less eager. His lifestyle had a habit of catching up with him, as Taylor's would do later on. This time it nearly killed him. He was drinking heavily and was almost certainly mainlining hard barbiturates. Meanwhile, Liz had her own problems. On location near Natchez, she had to struggle into period dresses weighing around 75 pounds and on one particularly hot day, she collapsed from hyperventilation. The production's doctor could not, by law, prescribe medication and none could be found. Liz was trying desperately to breathe and felt as if she were dying. Enter Clift, as if on cue, with a bottle of Demerol. Liz duly recovered. It was a routine that many more directors would have to get used to.

At one point, Dmytryk found Clift in his hotel room, so drunk and dead to the world that a cigarette had burned itself out between his fingers. Dmytryk later

Montgomery Clift would prove to be one of Liz's closest friends. She saved his life after a car
accident, but Clift would remain troubled by his drug addictions until his death by overdose

admitted that he conducted an illegal search of Clift's hotel room and found, 'a hundred containers' of every kind of drug and a leather case full of syringes and needles. When the company moved on to Danville, Kentucky, for more location shooting, Clift's behaviour worsened. To celebrate their first film together since making the classic *A Place In The Sun*, he and Liz went to the best restaurant in town, where Clift picked up a raw steak, dripping with butter, and wolfed it down like an animal to the disgust of hundreds of autograph hunters. He was later seen running naked through the residential part of Danville, much to the bemusement of the upper-crust residents. For the remainder of the production, a policeman was assigned to stand guard outside Clift's hotel room door to prevent him from leaving at night.

The mystery behind those famous eyes has puzzled critics and fans alike since Taylor first stepped in front of a camera

Liz was hardly an angel either. She was often late for shootings and was being wooed by producer Mike Todd during production. The film, which was cut to 166 minutes, was the last production sponsored by MGM's outgoing boss, Dore Schary, and it was not a monumental legacy to leave behind. It's a disjointed, sometimes brilliant film, but the rambling, unedited script and awkward dialogue prevent it from reaching classic status.

Liz wasn't unduly bothered. She had finally met the catch of her life in the person of the wildly charismatic film producer Mike Todd. Needless to say, Todd was everything that Michael Wilding (and indeed Montgomery Clift) had not been. Mike Todd was a classic larger-than-life entrepreneur. Tough, shrewd and possessed of enormous energy and chutzpah, Todd was louder, bigger and better than any screen hero with whom Liz had been previously paired. After the insufferably genteel Wilding, she was mesmerized by this man who couldn't stand still for a minute. Todd needed only four hours sleep at night and, through sheer will and ambition, he always got more or less what he wanted.

Todd's achievements, by any standard, were impressive. Born into a poor orthodox Jewish background, he had been a street-fighter, impresario, inventor and producer of Broadway plays, and was currently producing the most ambitious film of the moment, *Around The World In Eighty Days*. He had managed to poach almost every notable Hollywood star – apart from Liz Taylor – to appear in the film. If the truth be told, Todd's inflation of the Jules Verne classic, with David Niven as Phileas Fogg and the Mexican comedian, Cantinflas, as Passepartout, is an interminable travelogue, interspersed with sketches in which star-spotting at least affords some relief. There are cameos from hordes of luminaries ranging from Marlene Dietrich and Beatrice Lillie to Buster Keaton and Frank Sinatra. Period touches and the insane sense of empire-building in the old British Bulldog tradition keep the film bubbling along. However, whatever the plot's shortcomings, the film still contrives to be charming, eccentric and, technically at least, years ahead of its time.

Todd's career, however, shouldn't be dismissed lightly on the back of this one film. In the early 1950s he played an important role in Hollywood's rush for the wide-screen format in the wake of competition from the fast-expanding television industry. One of the original partners of the Cinerama Corporation, he sold his shares in the company in 1953 and announced the formation of the Magna Corporation in partnership with movie mogul, Joseph M Shenck, to exploit a 65 mm-wide screen process he named 'Todd-AO'. Magna's first production, *Oklahoma!* (1955), was a smash hit but its success was overshadowed by the spectacular box-office returns from the star-studded, multi-million dollar epic, *Around The World In Eighty Days*.

With two marriages behind him, Todd had made and lost several fortunes. After meeting Liz at a cocktail party on a yacht where a sexual chemistry ignited between them, Todd began to see her as a financial investment. To him, Liz wasn't just gorgeous, she was also a good career move. Mike didn't ask Liz to marry him. He more or less told her. Liz was bowled over by the sheer nerve of a man who had the endearing habit of plunging his hand down the front of her cleavage, once even when her parents were across the table. At last she felt she had a real man, someone who could make decisions, someone who could pay bills and, above all, someone who could provide excitement. Michael Wilding was fading into history.

Having played the part of so many Hollywood heroines who plumped for the exciting rogue and never got him, it's easy to see why Liz felt she had struck oil here. She wanted a man who could command her and Todd was more than equal to her frequent tantrums. Mike would fight back with equal ferocity, but he was also fiercely protective of her. In November 1956, after filing for divorce from Michael Wilding, Liz went on a Caribbean cruise with Mike Todd, on board Lord Beaverbrook's yacht. Climbing down a stairway, she slipped and landed on her coccyx. Todd whisked her off to an orthopaedic specialist at Harkness Pavilion in New York, where tests revealed that she had suffered crushed spinal discs. It was a five-hour, make-or-break operation.

According to Liz: 'Three discs were gone. They cut away all the dead bone right down to the nerve centre; they took bone from my hip, my pelvis and from a bone bank, and made little matchsticks and formed clusters that finally calcified and became one long column, about six inches long.' Every three hours the nurses rotated her to keep the newly constructed spinal column from sagging. Liz said that the pain was so excruciating she passed out. The fretful Mike hovered in a room next to hers like a caged bear. He bought paintings – a Renoir, a Pissarro and a Monet – to brighten her hospital room; he ordered meals for her from his favourite New York restaurant. One thing Mike probably didn't tell the waiting press was the fact that his 24-year-old fiancée, still legally married to Wilding, was pregnant. Although Liz recovered, she thought she had appendicitis and flew back to Los Angeles in December for an appendectomy, bringing the number of major operations she had undergone in less than a year to the astonishing total of three.

Wilding, decent as ever, agreed to a divorce and even flew to Mexico to facilitate the proceedings. On 2 February 1957, Liz married Mike Todd in Acapulco.

*Eddie Fisher, Liz Taylor and Mike Todd: Liz would end up marrying Fisher, Todd's
best man, when the charismatic entrepreneur died in a tragic air accident*

She actually had to be carried to the altar to make her vows after her spinal fusion
operation. It was a testament to the complete lack of passion in her marriage to
Wilding that she and her former husband were able to remain on amicable terms.
Once again, Liz told the waiting world that she was giving up her career to become
the perfect wife, as Mrs Mike Todd.

Strangely enough (and for the first time in one of her married lives), she suited
the role perfectly. Pleased, at last, to have the opportunity to escape from California
without having to shoot a film, she happily globetrotted after Todd, helping him to
promote his Oscar-winning picture, *Around The World In Eighty Days*, with a series of
spectacularly lavish parties. Although he was ostensibly using Liz, Todd dragged her
out of what Sheridan Morley calls 'the dark ages of old studio contracts, and
established her as one of the great showbiz attractions of the middle 1950s'.

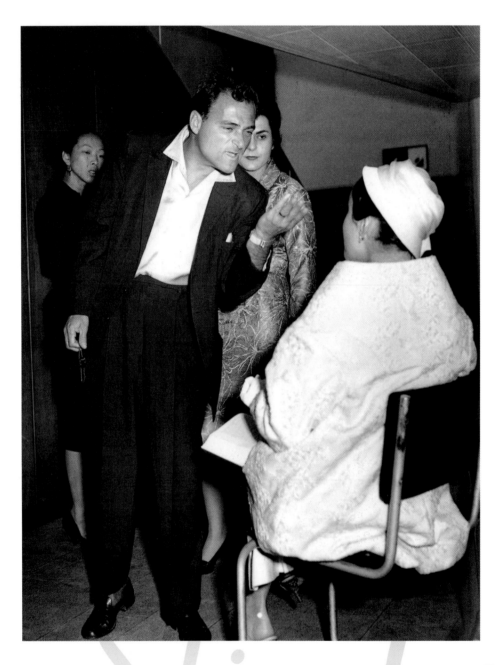

Mike Todd gives Liz a piece of his mind after they miss a flight to Nice. Todd wore his passions on his sleeve. He wasn't afraid of airing them in public

The immediate pay-off was a daughter – Elizabeth Frances Todd – born on 6 August 1957 by Caesarian. Difficulties with the birth, however, put paid to Liz's chances of ever bearing children again. She had to have tubal ligation. It was a grim shock for a young woman in her prime. There were more to follow. Mike was everything to Liz – friend, lover, husband, mentor and playmate, but, perhaps most significantly (and to the utter chagrin of the studios), he also became her agent.

Mike Todd was not a man to squander opportunities when they presented themselves, and Liz rapidly became his greatest asset. He was keen to secure lucrative one-off picture deals for her. Despite the success of *Around The World In Eighty Days*, Todd was far from financially secure. He was a consummate bluff merchant who borrowed and traded on his extraordinary talent for seeming to go places which promised lucrative returns. *Around The World* financed a lot of glamorous travel and some hugely expensive launch parties, but its popularity wasn't inexhaustible.

After her marriage to Todd, Taylor's fame escalated to the point where her life was now far more famous than her work. When Grace Kelly left Hollywood to marry Prince Rainier, MGM were desperate to get Liz and cast her in the film of the Tennessee Williams play, *Cat On A Hot Tin Roof*. Despite the tubal ligation, life had never been better for Liz. She finally had the right husband and the right part. Sadly, her happiness proved to be short-lived. On 22 March 1958, two weeks into the shooting of *Cat On A Hot Tin Roof*, Todd's private plane crashed into the New Mexico mountains, killing all on board. He was en route to New York for a dinner with the National Association of Theater Owners, at which he was to be named Showman of the Year. Ironically, the plane was named 'The Lucky Liz', after his wife. Todd's body was so badly burnt and mangled that he could only be identified by a ring. Once again, the world's sympathies were on Liz's side.

Arguably the greatest love of her life, Todd was the one man with whom Liz could most likely have sustained a happy marriage. The couple had so much in common: a need for love; a hatred of being alone. They had passionate tempers, a love of a good argument, foul language and a bawdy sense of humour. And they were also completely infatuated with each other. There were some mighty fights and plenty of tears, but that's to be expected in even the most robust of marriages. After Todd's death, a semi-hysterical Liz plunged into a depression from which many feel she has never actually recovered. In fact, she missed that fatal plane journey because, irony of ironies, she had a cold. This unhappy period in her life was dominated by drugs: sleeping pills, antidepressants and pills to counteract the effects of the sleeping pills.

Alleged drug abusers, such as Clift, were hardly ideal friends. Although the world shared her obvious, terrible grief, it was dismayed when Liz rapidly began to find solace in Eddie Fisher.

Although paralysed by bereavement, Liz began to show another dimension to her public character – an ability to endure and bounce back from tragedy. Although the funeral may have been a paparazzi nightmare, with photographers tearing the funeral cortège apart to get at Liz, the actress kept her cool. In the midst of all this sadness she was to prove herself the consummate professional on set. Cast by Richard Brooks in the MGM production of *Cat On A Hot Tin Roof*, Liz went on to give one of the greatest performances of her career.

Acting the part of Maggie, the sexually frustrated wife of Paul Newman's gay alcoholic Brick, provided a refuge from a reality that Liz wasn't ready to face. Her work kept her going, while off-set she was incapable of functioning properly. Critics loved and hated this movie, but none of them will ever forget what a breakthrough it was – in terms of film, as much as Liz Taylor's handling of it.

Censorship reared its prudish head when Richard Brooks and James Poe adapted Williams' steamy play for the screen. Set on a wealthy estate, the film charts how lust, greed, frustration and impotence tear apart a big Southern family. In his best role ever, Burl Ives' fierce patrician, Big Daddy, is dying of cancer but no one has the guts to tell him the truth about his condition. It's his sixty-fifth birthday and his obnoxious, boring, eldest son and their vulgar family have arrived to plague him like vultures. Who will get Big Daddy's sizeable inheritance? His childless, favourite son, Brick (Paul Newman) and his wife, Maggie (Liz) are at each other's throats. Maggie wants a child, not only to secure a chunk of Big Daddy's $10-million fortune, but also because she genuinely loves Brick. But Brick, half-crippled by a sporting accident, refuses to sleep with her while he seethes in alcoholic despondency over the suicide of his best friend (and homosexual infatuation), Skip.

Needless to say, all the gay references were removed for the screen. Newman had to play his part as a cripple, rather than as a man struggling with his own sexual identity. To his credit, he was able to infuse the character with enough between-the-lines emotions to get the message across without the wardens of the 1958 Production Code going berserk. Six Oscar nominations were awarded but, criminally, the film didn't pick up a single one. Taylor's sexy, distracted performance was favourably compared to Barbara Bel Geddes' recent stage appearance as Maggie. A cool exterior barely masked her seething emotions and the work engaged Liz enough to prevent certain nervous breakdown. It also injected enormous credibility

Liz's taste for jewellery and furs was legendary

A day at Epsom races: Liz and husband Mike Todd cross the finishing line hotly pursued by best friends, pop singer Eddie Fisher and his wife, Debbie Reynolds

into Taylor's career. Unlike Greta Garbo or Marilyn Monroe, Liz was not about to turn into a recluse even though she was now a single mother of three children in a severely diminished financial state. Mike Todd's wealth proved as illusory as everyone had suspected.

Ironically, the seeds of Taylor's next marriage were sown in her husband's death. Eddie Fisher was his best man and the go-between when Todd was wooing Liz. The teen idol and pop star was not just a great friend, but almost an adopted son to Todd. It seemed entirely natural to Liz that she should turn to him for support. Fisher was married to another young starlet, Debbie Reynolds (one of Liz's best friends), and their image was of a fairy-tale couple. In reality, Fisher's marriage to Reynolds had been falling apart for some time and he had always envied Todd his great love affair with a woman as exciting as Elizabeth. Now he was at her side, ready to console her.

Fisher proved the perfect escort and ideal comforter, being the nearest thing – apart from her daughter – that Liz had to Mike Todd. Eddie, also Jewish, loved the high life and, like Todd, was easily seduced by fame and glamour. With no respect for the widows liturgies of the time, which held that a widow should remain in purdah for a decade at least, Liz was observed to have recovered perversely quickly when she was seen at Fisher's far-flung concerts and publicly displayed herself on his arm. Once again, the tabloids took up arms against her.

It seemed that no sooner had Liz won the world's sympathy than she set about losing it. Less than six months after Todd's death, Liz and Eddie's affair was being endlessly chronicled in sanctimonious tabloid headlines and film fanzines. Middle America's sympathy for the grieving widow needed precious little prodding before it turned to disgust at the scarlet woman and professional home-wrecker. Debbie Reynolds made a meal of the wronged woman role. She was pictured at home with her baby and small child, looking not only virtuous, but positively saintly. Ironically, Reynolds' film hits of the time were *The Mating Game* and *It Started With A Kiss*.

Liz inadvertently put the seal on the matter by madly spilling all to her long-time confidante and supposed friend, the journalist Hedda Hopper, also known, with reason, as 'the Queen of the Gossips'. As Sheridan Morley astutely notes in his biography, Debbie had not made public the difficulties of her marriage to Eddie Fisher. Liz, as so often before, was just telling the truth as she saw it. But the article turned on a devastasting quote. Liz said to Hopper: 'What did you expect me to do, sleep alone?', which Hopper cheekily abbreviated to 'Mike's dead, I'm alive.' There was public uproar at the bluntness of Liz's defence. She was tactfully trying to say that Debbie and Eddie's marriage had never been a happy one; that she couldn't be expected to live the rest of her life as a nun, and that she had a right to a personal life. Hopper presented it in a somewhat different light.

After Hopper's mischievous behaviour, the moral outrage across the globe was almost palpable. 'Eddie-Debbie-Liz-biz' hate mail arrived by the sackload. Churchgoers claimed they would boycott all Fisher's concerts and Taylor's films. There was even a motion tabled in the House of Representatives to have Fisher and Taylor banned from the US on account of their undesirability. Amazingly, Liz did not seem unduly bothered by the public outrage. She had toughened up considerably since her first divorce and was not about to let anything get in the way of her new happiness. She was justifiably more upset about not getting an Oscar for her performance in *Cat On A Hot Tin Roof* and was half right in believing she lost because the panel disapproved of her private life. Ultimately, however, the gay subtext of Williams' play effectively shot the film's chances down.

Unprompted by Eddie, Liz even converted to the Jewish faith to be closer to him. (This promptly caused several Arab countries to ban her films.) Ironically, it was Eddie's rather than Liz's career which was damaged by their eventual marriage on 12 May 1959. Once again, Liz announced to the world that she would give up her career after her next two contracted films to completely devote herself to her new husband and young children.

After the couple's slating by the public, Eddie Fisher was no longer regarded as the dreamboat that he clearly thought he was. His concert bookings started to dry up. Pop music, anyway, was changing faster than he was able to. Added to this, he had no discernible talent for anything other than crooning, which became patently obvious when Liz managed to secure him a small part in *Suddenly Last Summer*, filmed in England a month after the wedding. Liz was to prove that, at least financially, any publicity is good publicity. Even hardened cynics had to agree that notoriety comes with fat compensations. The scandal did nothing to diminish the box-office success of *Cat On A Hot Tin Roof*. Against all the odds, Liz was voted the star that most movie-goers wanted to see.

More importantly of all, however, Liz was offered the chance to cement her reputation as a first-rank actress and one of Tennessee Williams' most important cinematic role-players when producer Sam Spiegel and director Joseph L Mankiewicz cast her in *Suddenly, Last Summer*. This bizarre, gamey and powerful film was the most sexually avant-garde commercial film production that Hollywood had yet produced. It daringly went far beyond the realms of 1950s' decency and out into a world that the average film-goer had no idea existed. The one-act play on which the film was based, consisted essentially of monologues by two women and was the second half of a Williams' double-bill collectively known as *The Garden District* (the first half was called *Something Unspoken*).

Williams and Gore Vidal expanded the play into an outrageous, melodramatic shocker, touching on madness, homosexual prostitution, incest, disease and cannibalism. Enough dysfunction, in other words, to sustain an American Lit seminar for years. Most of it, for obvious reasons, is indicated rather than shown.

In the film Montgomery Clift plays a brain surgeon who specializes in lobotomies in a tacky Louisiana State Hospital. Desperately in need of funds, Clift is despatched to Katharine Hepburn's rich millionairess to squeeze the funds from her

Liz Taylor and Eddie Fisher sign their marriage licence at 2.35pm, May 12, 1959.
Their relationship, which blossomed soon after Mike Todd's death, shocked the world

Only Liz Taylor could wear stilettos with a leopard-skin swim suit and get away with it

vast bank account. The unsavoury price he has to pay for this is to lobotomize Taylor's Catherine Holly, a girl disturbed after witnessing a nasty fatal accident that befalls Hepburn's beloved son, Sebastian, on a tour of Morocco. Recovering from the breakdown, Liz tells Clift enough for him to realize that Hepburn wants something concealed. It transpires that Sebastian was a predatory homosexual who would use his mother as bait to attract young boys, with whom he would then have his way. No longer attractive, Hepburn is swapped for her niece (Taylor), who unwittingly allows herself to be used in exactly the same way in Morocco. Sebastian's fatal accident has an almost hysterical touch of poetic justice about it. After routinely debauching poor, angry young men, they then turn on him like a pack of wolves and literally devour him.

It's extremely powerful stuff. The one-act material is stretched perilously thin, but it works for Hepburn as the incarnation of civilized depravity, and Taylor has rarely been more luminous as the psychologically scarred survivor. Hollywood had never seen the like before and wouldn't do so again until the late 1960s. Both Liz and Hepburn were nominated for Best Actress Oscars, but probably cancelled each other out in the final voting, allowing Simone Signoret to win for Jack Clayton's *Room At The Top*.

Suddenly, Last Summer was as deeply troubled a movie as it was troubling. Clift was working with no insurance because he had failed two medical examinations due to his drug habit. Hence his wooden, glassy-eyed performance: his memory and concentration were shot to pieces by the drugs. Both Spiegel and Mankiewicz wanted to replace him but, once again, Liz threatened to pull out of the film altogether if he was dropped. There were endless takes on Clift's long speeches, most of which had to be cut in half.

Hepburn clearly felt uneasy on the set. Her long-time secret lover, Spencer Tracy, was beginning to succumb to the illness which would claim him less than ten years later and Hepburn was distressed. The director Mankiewicz was suffering from a bad skin ailment that necessitated wearing gloves during the shooting. At the end of the shooting, once Mankiewicz assured Hepburn that she was no longer needed, she spat in his face because she didn't appreciate the way he treated her, Clift or anyone else. On a final odd note, Clift's boss in the film, the actor Albert Dekker, died shortly afterwards as a result of a weird sexual practice that involved a lot of bright paints and asphyxiation. He was found hanging from the ceiling, like a work of art.

During the shooting of the film Liz received a phone call from Fox's legendary producer, Walter Wanger, that would change her life. She was offered the part of

Cleopatra and jokingly asked for a $1 million fee against 10 per cent of the gross profits, plus script and location approval. To her amazement, he agreed. But Liz still owed MGM one more film from her fifteen-year contract and there was no way that the studio was going to let its most ungovernable daughter go without extracting a last pound of flesh. Flesh was the apposite word. With incredibly bad grace, Liz agreed to shoot *Butterfield 8*, a John O'Hara novel about a New York call girl with the delicious name of Gloria Wandrous, whose unhappy affair with a married man leads to her death in a car crash. The story, based on an unsolved murder case involving a New York flapper called Starr Faithfull, with whom O'Hara was obsessed, had long been on the MGM shelf.

O'Hara, never noted for taking kindly to criticism, was less than pleased at the way Liz rubbished his story as being cheap, commercial and in the worst possible taste, and her character as being a 'slut' and 'sick nymphomaniac'. Even the fact that Eddie Fisher was given a spear to hold during the film refused to placate Liz, who must have felt in some degree that the film was a public branding of her lifestyle. Neither O'Hara nor the critics thought much of the way in which the script writers, Charles Schnee and John Michael Hayes managed to turn the author's urban tragedy into a slick soap. Though decidedly weak, the film, fraught with sexuality and death, is saved by Taylor's performance, which, in spite of her truculence about the project, is one of her best. It tapped into the emerging era of guilt-free enjoyment of which Burton and Liz would soon become the apogee. The film struck a blow for the sisterhood, long before bra-burning and Germaine Greer got going, in it's depiction of whisky-drinking, sexually liberal woman. The crowning irony is that after being nominated for four years running for an Oscar, this is the picture that finally did it for Taylor.

Meanwhile the press still raged about the Fisher marriage. Years later in 1976, when she complained to a journalist that her life was becoming complicated and she wanted a bit of peace, the journalist, Glen Davis, replied: 'Oh, come now, Elizabeth, anyone can find peace but not many have it in them to carry off a really rip-snorting drama.' Rip-snorting is probably not the best phrase to use to describe the first few months of the greatest fiasco ever committed to film, namely *Cleopatra*.

By the time Fox had spent some $3 million building sets in Pinewood Studios, England and another million getting rid of the original director, Rouben Mamoulian, and buying Mankiewicz out of various directing commitments, *Cleopatra* was already showing all the signs of being a dangerously precarious prospect. Shooting started in the winter of 1960, just as thick fogs and rain looked to be setting in for the rest of

Liz in 1956: the year she made Giant *and* Raintree Country, *and started dating Mike Todd*

Liz in evening wear: all the better to show off her diamond ear rings

the millennium. Trying to recreate burning Roman and Egyptian suns was clearly a non-starter. To cap it all. Liz caught 'flu and the script was all over the place.

Shooting was abandoned until early 1961 when, on 4 March, a catastrophe unfolded that no one could have possibly predicted. Liz was rushed to the London Clinic with a lung congestion so severe that it threatened to kill her. She was so close to suffocating that she had to undergo a highly dangerous emergency operation. The double pneumonia contracted while filming *Butterfield 8* was compounded by a dose of Asiatic 'flu. Her respiratory system failed and she underwent a traumatic emergency tracheotomy, in which her throat was cut open and the lungs pumped free of fluid to enable her to breathe. She was declared clinically dead on four occasions. Following the operation, she contracted anaemia. For days the prognosis was grim. Eddie Fisher lost 15 pounds while agonizing by her bedside and, in a frantic transatlantic call, he sobbed: 'I think I'm going to lose my girl.' Liz later claimed that seeing Fisher beside her bed each time she regained consciousness gave her the will to live. She told an interviewer that she had been fascinated to read what the newspapers had written about her when they feared she would not survive pneumonia in 1961: 'I got the best notices of my life,' she answered wryly. Her imminent demise wrought an extraordinary effect on the press at large. Within a few days, she was no longer being written about as the overpaid, spoilt adulteress, but instead as the world's most glamorous woman, who had been through the eye of the needle and lived to tell the tale.

There is a peculiar truth about industries as fickle as motion pictures and the stage. The glue that holds the whole shebang together is finally the actors. And when one as prominent and valuable as Liz looks as though she may be stolen away in her prime, there is a weird, but highly palpable sense of unity. The myth kicks in. It happened to James Dean as surely as it happened to the Brazilian racing driver, Ayrton Senna, and to Diana, Princess of Wales. Enmities take second place to tragedies.

It happened to Liz too. People who had shamelessly slated her were quick to forgive and forget. Although Liz managed to survive her health scares, many of her contemporaries died in tragic circumstances. Carl Switzer was shot, Montgomery Clift and Marilyn Monroe died of drug overdoses, James Dean died in a car crash, Rock Hudson succumbed to Aids, and there was still the premature death of Richard Burton (from alcohol abuse) to come.

As she lay in the London Clinic, tons of mail, miracle cures and flowers arrived from all parts of the globe and people prayed for her recovery. When Liz recovered in time for the Oscars in April, it would have been churlish not to give her the priceless statuette for which she had been nominated so many times. As Sheridan Morley says, even Debbie Reynolds acknowledged that she had voted for Liz out of relief for her medical survival.

One of the most notable features of Liz's extraordinary story has been how prone she is to accidents and tragedies. Her life has been blitzed by illness, drugs, alcohol and a fistful of life-threatening hospitalizations. What is frequently underestimated is the extent to which these misfortunes preyed on Liz's emotional and psychological well-being. Nowadays, she is always keen to stress how lucky she is to have lived so long and seen so much, and how personal set-backs have stiffened her resolve in fighting for her Aids charities. This is true. But it's equally true that problems with her health stemmed as much from her own propensity to addiction – a life-long weakness. It became easier for Liz to live the life of a hypochondriac than deal with pain, and, at some stages of her career, real life itself.

An inventory of her health problems makes for remarkable reading. Liz was born with a spine defect in 1932. In 1942 she broke her foot while filming *Lassie Come Home*. Studio files show that the young starlet called in sick at least twice a month. She compacted her spine in 1944 when she fell off a horse during the filming of *National Velvet*. Ironically, she starred in *Cynthia* (1947) as a sickly teenager whose frailties were intensified by overprotective parents. 'I think she might have carried her ill and ailing on-camera role into real life,' commented an insider, unaware of what an understatement this would later prove to be throughout Liz's career.

When a pimple marred the porcelain complexion of the 15-year-old Liz, at a time when she was being mooted as one of the most desirable women in the world, top dermatologists were consulted. A minor cough demanded a thoracic investigation. When she stepped on a nail, Taylor was whisked to the studio hospital immediately by ambulance. A cold could hold up production on a major film and in 1952 the studios panicked when her weight dropped to 7 stone, 2 pounds.

Huge chunks of Liz's career have been spent collapsing and recuperating. Directors, such as George Stevens on *Giant*, used to think that her delicate constitution was mostly put on. However, history begs to differ. Taylor has always been more susceptible than most to illness. Her insurance premiums on film sets were staggering.

In later years, she developed a drug list as long and convoluted as Elvis Presley's. And in many ways she shares similar neurotic needs to those of her close friend, Michael Jackson. There has been a high price to pay for her success. Fame shines brightest next to mortality and the tragedy of a dying star focuses the public's

*Liz sharing an intimate meal with Stanley Donen, the dashing director who briefly captured
the heart of the actress during his 1952 production of* Love Is Better Than Ever

Liz's chemistry with the camera was no less priceless than the diamonds she wore

imagination like no other. In this century, Princess Diana was the greatest example of this phenomenon. In 1959 Liz nearly played the same role when she almost died before the cameras started rolling for *Cleopatra*.

When Liz finally recovered and left hospital to pick up her Oscar for *Butterfield 8*, her car was besieged by rejoicing fans. It was left to Shirley MacLaine, who had also been nominated, for her part in *The Apartment*, to comment acidly that she had lost out to a tracheotomy. The outward drama of Liz's life, however, could not disguise the fact that her marriage to Fisher was quickly losing its initial fizz. Eddie was, by this stage (like Michael Wilding before him), slotting into the familiar role of Mr Elizabeth Taylor.

But with the renewed appetite for Liz still fresh in people's minds, it looked as if, against all the odds, Fox could salvage *Cleopatra*, if not her marriage. However, it was clearly going to be done on Taylor's terms. Even Liz felt inspired. She renewed her commitment to the project with an enthusiasm that she hadn't displayed since her first films for MGM in a career now nearly twenty years old. And she was also about to meet the man who would have the greatest single influence on her life: he was an aspiring Welsh actor called Richard Burton.

CHAPTER III

CARRY ON DOWN THE NILE

lizabeth Taylor was about to turn 30 when she began the affair with Richard Burton which the press famously dubbed 'Le Scandal'. On her fourth marriage, already a legend and able to command a million dollars a picture, Liz actually had more box-office pulling power than any of the films she graced. But for all her screen triumphs, her greatest role in the 1960s would be as the lover and wife of Richard Burton.

As a couple, they were in a league of their own. Even when they weren't together, they were still heavily involved in each other's triumphs and misfortunes. For the first time ever, Liz found herself in a relationship where the accumulation of material wealth and heavy spending were habits worth aspiring to. For better or worse, both parties managed to convey the decade's idea of glamour: passion, money, bad taste and conspicuous consumption. Theirs became the yardstick by which all famous affairs, famous marriages and famous excesses were measured, and continue to be measured to this day. The couple were far more interesting than any storyline that Hollywood could dream up. Their boozy, decadent lifestyle provided a template for rock stars and cheaper imitators for the next twenty years.

Life constantly imitated art during Liz's life, but never more so than when she met Richard Burton on the set of *Cleopatra*. It was entirely fitting that two of the world's mightiest egos should meet on the set of the most expensive movie ever made – a movie that encapsulated the complete absurdity of Hollywood.

Originally estimated at a modest $3 million, the budget for *Cleopatra* escalated out of all control during the two and a half years that it took to complete the production.

Liz the dreamer found the greatest love of her life on the set of Cleopatra

Cleopatra in heels? Liz brought more than a modern touch to the Queen of the Nile

The final cost was some $40 million, which today equates to the stupendous sum of $300 million, a full $100 million more than *Titanic*. The movie nearly destroyed Twentieth Century Fox. In fact, it's a miracle that it didn't and even now, survivors from the movie discuss the making of it almost as if they are discussing a paranormal experience. The director, Joseph Mankiewicz, famously described it as: 'the toughest three pictures I ever made … conceived in a state of emergency, shot in confusion and wound-up in a blind panic.' Although *Cleopatra* ended up turning a small profit and winning modest critical acclaim, the after-effects on many of its principals were grim. Mankiewicz never again attained the brilliance and fecundity of his late 1940s' and 1950s' peak, during which he pulled off the still-unmatched feat of winning four Oscars in two years. He made only three more features, concluding with the magnificent *Sleuth* in 1972, and then spent his final twenty-one years disillusioned, 'finding reasons not to work' (in the words of his son).

The film's producer, 68-year-old legend Walter Wanger, never made another movie again. He had hoped that *Cleopatra* would be the crowning point in his distinguished career, which began in 1921 when he persuaded Paramount to put Rudolph Valentino in *The Sheik*. When *Cleopatra* opened, the new Fox president, Darryl F Zanuck took him off the film as he was targeted as the prime suspect in the whole sorry mess.

By the time Burton arrived in Rome in September 1961, a year and $7 million dollars had already been wasted, with a mere ten minutes of film in the can. Not a foot of it was remotely usable and Liz wasn't even featured. The director, Rouben Mamoulian, now a broken man, resigned and Mankiewicz took over. Mamoulian's efforts to shoot *Cleopatra* at Pinewood Studios outside London in the middle of winter were a comedy of errors, capped only by Elizabeth's near death.

Liz, of course, survived. In some of the publicity stills for *Cleopatra* you can see the tracheotomy scar snaking an inch and a half down her neck on one side of her windpipe. Although calamitous, two good things actually came out of the episode. First, Mankiewicz had six more months to try to get the sprawling script into some sort of shape while Liz recovered from her operation. And secondly, the publicity generated by the newspapers and the subsequent Oscar for *Butterfield 8* transformed Liz's box office potential. More than any of her films (even *Cleopatra*), this act of survival against all the odds moved her up from the A list of Hollywood actors to the ranks of Hollywood royalty.

Mankiewicz decided to scrap Mamoulian's original footage and reconstruct the movie from the beginning. A sunnier climate was needed and Cinecitta just outside

Rome was booked for the production. Mankiewicz also decided to replace everybody apart from Elizabeth herself, so a new cast and crew was hired and a second enormous set had to be built. (The old Pinewood sets were finally colonized by the *Carry On* team, who enterprisingly improvised their own version of the story – *Carry On Cleo*.)

To replace Peter Finch and Stephen Boyd (the original Caesar and Antony respectively), Mankiewicz pursued Trevor Howard and Marlon Brando. Brando seemed a natural because he had played Mark Antony in the director's acclaimed 1953 adaptation of Shakespeare's *Julius Caesar*. Neither actor was available, so the director set his sights on Rex Harrison and Richard Burton (Burton was receiving wide acclaim on Broadway in *Camelot* at the time).

Spyros Skouras, Greek tycoon and president of Fox until Darryl Zanuck wrested control away from him in 1962, hated both choices. Skouras claimed that Harrison had never made a profitable movie for Fox and Burton 'doesn't mean a thing at the box office'. In fact, Burton, a dashing 36-year-old product of a poor Welsh mining family, was perceived in Hollywood to be a great stage actor whose film career had never really taken off.

Mankiewicz insisted on his two choices of actor and he was also determined to rewrite the script. Although Skouras gave way on this, he forced Mankiewicz to push ahead with filming before the script was finished as he didn't want to lose any more money on the movie through delays. Mankiewicz ended up directing by day and writing at night. To do this, he kept himself going by taking amphetamines and nearly killed himself with overwork in the process.

Liz herself was by now an enormous cost. She demanded another million dollars to restart the film in Rome and her expenses were enormous. Fox had to install her in a fifteen-room villa outside Rome with a large entourage which included her own private physician. Following her recent illness, she was almost uninsurable and the producers were terrified of further health problems. If Liz didn't appear in the film, there would be no film and endless debt. As a result, they did everything in their power to humour their star, employing her husband, Eddie Fisher, on a substantial $150,000 retainer to act as nursemaid and make sure she got to the set on time. Although an utter professional in front of the camera, Liz was as capable of bad behaviour off-screen as any Hollywood star. Her demands about the script and about how she was to be treated tried the patience of both husband and studio.

In a typical piece of mismanagement, Burton arrived in Rome four months before he was actually needed. Casting was done on a wing and a prayer. A flurry of phone

Liz resplendent on one of the extraordinary sets created for Cleopatra

Elizabeth Taylor and Richard Burton talking through a scene with Cleopatra *director Joseph L Mankiewicz*

calls brought actors such as Hume Cronyn, Martin Landau and Carroll O'Connor from America, and Kenneth Haigh, Robert Stephens and Michael Hordern from England. But when the actors arrived in Rome they discovered half-finished sets and incomplete wardrobes, not to mention an exhausted writer-director who hadn't yet written their parts.

All manner of bizarre blunders occurred, due largely to the pace demanded by a nervous Fox studios. The beach at Torre Astura, where art director John De Cuir's massive replica of Alexandria was under construction, turned out to be peppered with live mines left over from World War II. A $22,000 mine-dredging expense was added to the ledger. Next to the set was a NATO firing range, which disrupted shooting while various military regiments re-enacted the Somme. And because Italy had no facilities for processing the Todd-AO film stock designed by Liz's late husband, rushes had to be sent all the way to Hollywood and then back to Rome before the director could actually view them.

De Cuir's sets were grandiose and magnificent, but also unmanageably large. A fake Roman Forum, costing $1.5 million, dwarfed the real one just up the road and the amount of steel tubing required to support it exacerbated a country-wide shortage. The sheer size and disorganization of the project made it easy for the Italians brought in to construct the Forum to overcharge the production company. Later on, Liz had a chance to see the studio's breakdown of financial wastage: 'They had $3 million under 'miscellaneous' and $100,000 for paper cups. They said I ate twelve chickens and forty pounds of bacon every day for breakfast. What?'

And still the costs piled up. As a bout of torrential rain prevented shooting for much of autumn 1961, at a cost of between $40,000 and $75,000 for every day that was lost, many of the principal actors realized they were going to be in Rome until well into 1962. At one point Skouras approached Burton to see if he would mind if the movie ended with Caesar's assassination, thereby cutting out half the plot and roughly 95 per cent of Antony's part. Richard was succinct about this: 'I'll sue you until you're puce,' he told him.

During this time Liz and Richard first got to know one another and by the time they did their first scene in front of the cameras, they had fallen very much in love. Liz was terrified Richard would lord his stage ability over her. However, he was grievously hung over and so nervous that he had forgotten his lines and had to have her steady his coffee cup to get it to his lips. 'He was probably putting it on,' Liz commented later. 'He knew it would get me.'

Born Richard Jenkins, the twelfth of thirteen children in an impoverished Welsh mining family, Burton was raised by his schoolteacher, Philip Burton (the surname is a coincidence), who spotted his talent at an early age and trained him for a stage career. Richard did not disappoint his tutor and rose quickly to become a name in the theatre. He was tipped to be the next Laurence Olivier and was considered to be one of the finest actors of his generation. Burton never made any secret of his utter contempt for the film industry, but he couldn't resist the money to be made.

Richard arrived in Rome independently wealthy but desperately eager for more. He left his long-suffering wife, Sybil, and their two daughters in London and appeared to be trailing his latest flame, a beautiful 22-year-old dancer. Sybil Burton was mostly unfazed by her husband's casual flings. However, although he had had plenty of affairs in the past, Liz would prove to be less accommodating. Burton's reputation as a womanizer was already well-known and Elizabeth adamantly did not want to be another notch on his belt. 'I'll be the one leading lady he doesn't get,' she claimed. Nor was Richard taken with the idea of Elizabeth Taylor. He described her as a 'fat little tart' and her husband as a 'busboy'. Dismissively associating Liz with Hollywood, he also assumed that she couldn't act to save her life.

He was right about one thing, however. By this time, Eddie Fisher was little more than a busboy. He was regarded as an inconvenience, who hung around the set where he wasn't wanted or even particularly liked. Fisher's career had taken a serious downturn since his marriage to Liz. The more obsequious Eddie became, the more Liz started to dislike him. Eddie continued to blindly court her approval, run her errands and probably provoked a lot of her appalling moods.

It is quite possible that by then, Liz had already strayed from the marriage bed to be with journalist and writer Max Lerner (one of the few members of the press who stood up for her later on). In any case, Liz later claimed that the Fisher marriage was clearly a mistake. While Eddie was given the thankless job of trying to contain Liz's excesses on *Cleopatra*, Richard was holding court in what became known as 'Burton's Bar'. In his self-described capacity as nurse, Fisher took exception to the influence the Welshman's prodigious boozing and earthy *joie de vivre* were having on Liz, who had grown tired of her husband's predilection for dining in. Burton was all for staying up late, getting drunk and to hell with the consequences. 'Remember,' says one Hollywood insider, 'Elizabeth was a very self-indulgent person … a sensualist who'd just been confronted with possible death and was probably rebounding from it by tasting as much life as possible.' They were, after all, in Rome at the time of Fellini's *La Dolce Vita* and Burton and Taylor were by no means the only people to feel this way.

Liz loved Burton's irreverence, his wicked stories and bawdy humour. When he tricked Fisher by swapping her empty glass with a full one at the bar, she thought: 'I absolutely adore this man.' Richard not only shared the machismo, wit and confidence of her other great love, Mike Todd, but he was also a wonderful actor and something of an intellectual. His ability to recite poetry (notably Dylan Thomas) and his love and knowledge of literature deeply impressed Liz after the shallowness of Hollywood.

Stepping out for some light shopping in one of her more revealing ensembles

Is this the face that launched a thousand writs? Liz looking serene in one of the most troubled movies ever made

Although physically short and blighted by a pockmarked face, Burton's sex appeal was legendary. He was a combination of ravaged good looks, a wonderfully deep, resonant voice and a crumpled charm, which those women on whom he chose to focus found irresistible. Elizabeth claims that the moment she fell in love with him was during that first morning-after scene when Richard was so dehydrated. In other words, she probably fell for his vulnerability and, in the classic motherly way that some women adopt, wanted nothing more than to help look after him. For all the chutzpah and cynicism about Hollywood and Taylor's place in it, Richard was deeply attracted to her, if not a little in awe. He was also, suprisingly, taken aback by how good a screen actress she was.

'When the camera starts rolling,' he said, 'she turns on the magic and you can't believe your eyes.' But what really inflamed his desire was seeing her naked in one of the bath scenes. 'That ought to be good for about $20 million on its own,' he joked. They began filming together on 22 January 1962. Within a few days everybody on the set realized they were not just playing Antony and Cleopatra. The producer – Walter Wanger – wrote in his diary: 'There comes a time during the making of a movie when the actors become the characters they play … This happened today … It was quiet and you could almost feel the electricity between Liz and Burton'.

Four days later Mankiewicz asked Wanger to come to his room at the Grand Hotel. 'I've been sitting on a volcano all alone for too long,' he said. 'There are some facts that you ought to know. Liz and Richard are not just playing Antony and Cleopatra.' This was the scandal that the hordes of paparazzi who had come to Rome were waiting for. News of a split in the Fisher marriage spread like wildfire, reporters flocked to the set and the way in which the film's budget was spiralling out of control simply added more rocket fuel. Paparazzi staked out every move that the famous couple made. They each tried to quash the rumours by denying their affair, claiming to both be happily married, but the game was already over.

Burton was genuinely bemused by all the furore. Several first-hand accounts support the idea that he began his dalliance with Taylor with only short-term pleasures in mind. Fox publicist Jack Brodsky recalls the actor's genuine surprise to find himself in the middle of both an intense affair and an international incident. 'He said to me,' says Brodsky, '"It's like fucking Khruschev! I've had affairs before – how did I know the woman was so fucking famous?"'

Burton's status was transformed overnight from respected Welsh nobody to international megastar. Laurence Olivier felt strongly enough, or perhaps jealous enough, to grill Richard on whether he really wanted to be the greatest stage actor of his generation or preferred to be just a household name. Burton responded that he wanted both. His market value had doubled overnight and Olivier was right to be uneasy about it. While Richard boasted to friends on site about his latest conquest – 'I just fucked Liz Taylor in the back of her Cadillac,' – he was becoming increasingly unnerved by the consequences. The lives of two spouses and six children were thrown into turmoil by this *fou d'amour* and they were swamped by all the publicity. Elizabeth was denounced by the Vatican for 'moral vagrancy' and they questioned her ability to be a fit mother. This was particularly upsetting for Liz as she had just adopted a German baby girl (Maria) with Eddie Fisher.

The producers, justifiably worried about the massive surge of media interest, tried to reason with their stars. Ironically, when the film was completed, they tried to sue the couple for $15 million for attempting to sabotage the whole project with bad press and lack of professionalism. Eddie Fisher suffered the ultimate humiliation when he phoned Liz from New York, in a room full of reporters, and asked her to deny the rumours. Far from pouring oil on troubled waters, Liz promptly claimed that the stories from the rumour mills were true. That was the last contact she had with Eddie for a couple of years and an acrimonious divorce blossomed. Richard found it much more difficult to leave his wife. Sybil had been loyal, faithful and immensely tolerant of his numerous affairs. She did not deserve to be finished with in such an underhand, highly public manner. There were also his two beloved daughters to consider. Richard doted on them, particularly his eldest child, Kate. His youngest daughter had been born with severe learning difficulties – a sad fact that only served to increase his undoubted feelings of guilt at the prospect of abandoning them both. For a year Richard vacillated back and forth, tossed on the horns of dilemma, unable to make up his mind, while trying to find ways to keep both women happy. Elizabeth apparently even contemplated the idea of becoming a full-time mistress, rather than destroy his family life.

Eventually, Richard summoned up the courage to tell Liz that the affair was over and he left for a short trip to Paris to play a small part in Darryl Zanuck's Normandy epic, *The Longest Day*. 'Total rejection,' wrote Wanger in his diary, 'came sooner than expected.' On 17 February, Liz was rushed to Salvator Mundi Hospital. The official explanation was food poisoning, but the truth of the matter was that Elizabeth had taken an overdose of the prescription sedative, Seconal. She claimed the overdose resulted from her hysterical state rather than a suicide attempt, which seems to be quite believable in the circumstances. Despite her propensity for pills, Liz wasn't the type to give up the ghost so easily, but she wasn't beyond a dramatic gesture or two.

Liz on her throne — worth every cent of her record-breaking million-dollar contract

The trappings of power: Liz at her most regal

Burton and Fisher promptly flew back to Rome. In the aftermath, all the aggrieved parties tried to carry on as before. Eddie threw a thirtieth birthday party for his wife and Richard told the world that he had no intention of leaving Sybil.

Inevitably, the pretence backfired on both sets of couples. Richard began drinking heavily. He was torn between his increasing love for Elizabeth, the enormous career prospects brought to him by the affair, and his guilt about the family that he abandoned at home when he travelled to work on films. It seemed beyond his power to stop his affair with Elizabeth while the two of them were smouldering on the set of *Cleopatra* and passionately embracing in the film's many love scenes. Even when they weren't filming together, Liz hung around the set and kept a close watch on her new leading man. Tired of skulking around, they decided to appear together in public.

The scandal reached its height when the couple took off for a romantic weekend in Portofino without any security and no warning. They must have been mad. They were swiftly hounded by swarms of paparazzi. 'It was like hell,' says Liz. 'There was no place to hide, not in this tiny cottage we had rented. When we were driving somewhere, they ran us into a ditch by jumping in front of the car.' Few could have predicted the fall-out or the immense cost of that weekend. Richard and Liz embarked on the first of their many violent quarrels. Liz came back with a black eye and misshapen nose and it was twenty-two days before she could start work again, at a cost to Fox of $250,000.

The difference in class, intellect and egos was beginning to make itself felt at a physical level that shocked them both. The pressure-cooker atmosphere was getting to them. And yet, though the relationship was often volatile, they stuck together like two partners in a *crime passionelle*. Was it the illicit nature of their love, or the sheer animal magnetism they felt for each other? Perhaps both. During April and May of 1962, the affair was the favoured front-page newspaper material as opposed to coverage of the Mercury-Atlas space missions and US–Soviet tensions leading up to the Cuban missile crisis. A congresswoman from Georgia, Iris Blitch, called on the Attorney General to block Taylor and Burton from re-entering the country 'on the grounds of desirability'. The complicity of the Vatican in slating Liz nearly undid her resolve to film Cleopatra's entrance into Rome, the centrepiece of the entire movie. Mankiewicz addressed the problem by devising the most lavish spectacle possible. Six thousand Italian extras had been hired for the scene. Liz expected an impromptu stoning, but the extras neither booed nor, for the most part, shouted 'Cleopatra!' They cheered and screamed 'Leez!, Leez!'

Cleopatra opened at the Rivoli Theater in New York to mixed reviews. The *New York Times* called it 'one of the great epic films of our day'. Most other newspapers were not so kind. The film appears lavish, beautiful and horribly expensive. Taylor's Cleopatra is a seething harridan, but her interpretation is extremely effective. Her dream of ruling the empire is believable, unlike her sexual relationship with Rex Harrison's Caesar. There is also a noticeable inconsistency in Taylor's physical appearance. At times she is slim and youthful and then at others, fleshy and heavily made-up around the eyes. Rex Harrison's Caesar gets all the good lines. Burton spends most of the film in a nostril-flaring state of rage, marching around Alexandria in a mini-toga. Unfortunately for him, Mark Antony's role suffered the worst cuts as the film was sliced down from over six hours to a modest 243 minutes for the opening night version. It was never the runaway success that Fox, at one time, dreamed it might be, but neither was it the complete turkey many cynics expected and even hoped for. A year after its release it was in the list of the top ten grossers of all time. In 1966, when Fox sold the television rights to ABC for $5 million, *Cleopatra* passed the break-even mark. By then, the studio had saved its skin financially with *The Sound Of Music*, which was released the year before and cost a paltry $8 million to make. (In fact, it went on to gross $100 million.)

The legacy of *Cleopatra* abides. Recently, with the support of the Mankiewicz family and Fox's current studio chief, Bill Mechanic, archivists have laboured to reconstruct a six-hour director's cut. Missing footage has been supplied by private collectors. Other bits of the film have been discovered in a mile-deep underground storage facility in Kansas. Movie buffs have also noticed that Charlton Heston used chunks from Mankiewicz's footage to flesh out his 1972 vanity production of *Antony And Cleopatra*.

The wrap party for the film unleashed a tornado of writs and counter-writs. Taylor and Burton sued Fox for their proper share of the gross profits. Fox sued Taylor and Burton for breach of contract, citing Taylor as 'suffering herself to be held up to scorn, ridicule and unfavourable publicity as a result of her conduct'. Wanger sued Skouras and Zanuck for breach of contract and Fox sued Wanger in return on the same grounds. Skouras contemplated a libel suit against Wanger for the way in which he was portrayed in the 1963 book, *My Life With Cleopatra*. He also issued another libel suit against Fox's publicists for the way in which he came across in Brodsky and Weiss's book, *The Cleopatra Papers*. By the end of the decade, all these actions were resolved.

Speaking after the trauma of the writs, Liz said: 'It wasn't a disaster for me because of my overtime. The suit against me was bigger than the suit against Richard, which

*Between two minds: Liz's relationship with Julius Caesar (Rex Harrison) would
soon be turned upside down by the arrival of Mark Antony (Richard Burton)*

The extraordinary larger-than-life-size sets for Cleopatra *were the making, and nearly the breaking, of the film*

infuriated him. But the whole action from Twentieth Century Fox amounted to $75 million. Then a theatre chain joined in and said the publicity of our romance had kept the audience away from the cinema. So we fought. Instead of winning that astronomical figure, which was so ridiculous – who has that kind of money except governments? – we did depositions for ten months and settled out of court and won $2.5 million. But it was finally getting to my stomach. After days full of depositions and these awful questions, I'd go home and be sick. So rather than fight it out all the way – and it could have been endless, it could have been years – we settled out of court, but won.'

Liz grew more voluptuous as her box office appeal climbed

ELIZABETH TAYLOR THE ILLUSTRATED BIOGRAPHY

It was during the making of *Cleopatra* that Liz truly transcended the label of movie star and became, once and for all, Elizabeth Taylor, the protagonist in a still-running melodrama of star-crossed romance, exquisite jewellery and emergency hospitalizations. 'It was probably the most chaotic time of my life. That hasn't changed,' says Liz, who seldom discusses the *Cleopatra* experience publicly. 'It was fun and it was dark – oceans of tears, but some good times too.'

For Hollywood, *Cleopatra* represented the exact moment when the sanitized star package ceased to be swallowed by the general public at face value. It was the time when every person on the street became an industry insider. The modern concept of the troubled production – *Waterworld, Ishtar, Heaven's Gate* – started here, even though none of these films ever came close to matching the sheer madness of the most expensive movie ever made.

Filming complete, Richard returned once more to his wife and Liz, for the first time in years, had no man in her life.

By the time the credits started rolling on Cleopatra, *Richard and Liz were the most glamorous scandal in the world*

CHAPTER IV

IN A LEAGUE OF THEIR OWN

y the time that filming of *Cleopatra* finally came to an end, Richard Burton and Elizabeth Taylor found themselves in the enviable position of being far more sought after together than they had ever been singly. Scripts, roles and lucrative offers poured in. Although Richard enjoyed his new-found status and the dollar signs it promised, he felt deeply uneasy about the thought of selling his artistic credibility for financial gain. Another part of his soul ached with the damage that the world's most famous affair had wreaked on both his wife and his family.

When Richard finally agreed to divorce Sybil at the beginning of 1963, he appeared to be destined for a nervous breakdown. In a classic case of role reversal, Liz acted as a nursemaid. The effect of this 'Faustian pact' with Hollywood and Liz had a terribly corrosive effect on Richard's conscience, eventually launching him on prolonged bouts of destructive behaviour. Many of his biographers and close relations are understandably convinced that Richard's personal problems arose in large part because he could never square his desires with his guilt at what he had done. That may well have been the case.

However, the powerful lure of box-office success, impossible fame and untold wealth had an uncanny hold on Richard's self-esteem, his ego and vanity. By the time he had any time to weigh up the consequences, he was well and truly in over his head. Before *Cleopatra* went on general release, Liz and Richard were already scheduled to star in *The VIPs*, a Terence Rattigan screenplay set at London Airport. The point of making the movie was obviously aimed at cashing in on the enormous

Liz relaxing during a stop at Jersey airport en route to Nice. Quarantine laws were more relaxed then

Where to now darling? Richard and Liz on the high road

public interest provoked by the couple. Naturally, the producers were nervous about media fatigue, but they wildly underestimated the magnetism of their stars. *The VIPs*, which beat *Cleopatra* to the big screens, grossed five times more than it cost to make.

The movie storyline charts the various problems and involvements of a group of wealthy people who are stranded in an airport terminal when their planes are grounded by thick fog. Script standards are typified by the episode in which a devoted secretary, Maggie Smith, persuades millionaire Richard Burton to write a cheque for a vast sum of money to save her boss (Rod Taylor) from ruin. Despite its corniness, the film drew reasonable performances from Taylor and Burton, with memorable cameos from the redoubtable Margaret Rutherford, Dennis Price and Orson Welles.

After finishing the film, Liz, who was now in the middle of the long and tedious process of being sued by Twentieth Century Fox over her contract for *Cleopatra*, didn't act again for another two years. Happy for the meantime to concentrate on fuelling Richard's long-frustrated ambition, she devoted herself to following her husband from set to set. It was almost as if Liz was happily waiting for Richard to catch up in terms of screen credibility and the stellar fees both were commanding.

Richard duly obliged. He was clearly on a roll and despite whatever personal misgivings he may have felt about quality, seemed to be enjoying himself. The tone was set by Peter Glenville's production of *Becket* (the version by Jean Anouilh), where Richard played the eponymous Archbishop of Canterbury in battle with Peter O'Toole's Henry II over the spiritual soul of England. It was a period romp, off the set as much in front of the cameras.

When the film wound up, Richard and Liz travelled to Mexico City so that he could begin shooting John Huston's epic *Night Of The Iguana*. Arriving at the airport at the start of the new film, the couple got their first real taste of the public mobbings that would haunt them for their rest of their lives together. During a series of ugly, hysterical scenes, Liz was severely manhandled and an enraged Richard resorted to his fists. The fans didn't want a simple view of the happy couple, they wanted a piece of them, literally. It nearly ruined what was to become a long love affair with Mexico. Despite the trauma of their arrival, Liz and Richard enjoyed some of their happiest days in a small village close to the shoot. In fact, they ended up buying the hacienda they were renting. Today, dedicated fans can pay to take a tour around the house, peer into the huge bath and walk around the enormous lounge and veranda bar overlooking Puerto. You can actually rent the house in high season, play pool and table tennis as the Burtons did, and even read their junk novels, which line the shelves in every room. For most people, it's probably the closest they will ever get to the stars.

Richard plays a fallen priest on the rebound from a major sex scandal in this superb Tennessee Williams script, which brought together Deborah Kerr, Ava Gardner and Sue (*Lolita*) Lyon. He played his role brilliantly, despite the fact that he was drinking a lot, even by his standards. The shoot itself was straightforward. John Huston, the director, treated the play with respect rather than reverence and even found places in which to inject his own sly humour.

Liz would apparently arrive at the set every day, wearing a different sexy outfit, with a hot meal she had had prepared for Richard – who didn't seem to mind this daily ritual of public seduction, or, indeed, Liz's obvious possessiveness. In fact, he positively relished the attention she lavished on him. He had given up so much in his life when he left his wife that Liz had become his whole world. It wasn't just the stability of his first marriage that he had lost: Richard ended up giving Sybil everything that he owned and had scrupulously saved up for throughout his entire career, apart from a house in Celigny, Switzerland. What money was left over, he gave to his family in Wales. This wasn't complete charity, however: he knew that marriage to Liz (and the fees he could now command) would more than replenish his bank balance within a year.

Elizabeth's acrimonious divorce to Eddie Fisher finally came through on 6 March 1964, just in time for Richard to make that famous curtain call announcement about their impending wedding at the end of *Hamlet* in Toronto. It crowned what proved to be a difficult transition back to top-class stage acting again. Burton hadn't been on stage for several years. He was out of shape and extremely nervous about one of the most demanding stage roles ever written. Not only that, the play was directed by one of the greatest Hamlets of the century, John Gielgud, who here favoured a surprisingly modern production. Against all the cynical predictions, Burton gave a dazzling performance as the prince.

Nine days later, the couple were married in Montreal (the only place, reportedly, where they could find a minister prepared to marry them). Liz, in true form, kept Richard waiting for forty-five minutes. Richard apparently swore himself into a muck sweat. He was never one for niceties – a defence mechanism, as much as anything else, in case he caught himself taking the world too seriously. As ever in his interviews and in the public eye, he was full of coarse bravado about Liz. Once the rings were exchanged a certain relief settled over the couple, and Liz – and Richard – watchers the world over.

No one, of course, could have predicted that the Burtons were to enjoy another five marriages between them, including a second to each other. This particular one lasted a decade and was the longest, most substantial and meaningful of all Liz's partnerships. It goes without saying that they experienced more passion, love and bonding than many marriages of greater length.

Despite the cruel reviews for *Cleopatra* that continued to trickle in ('Over-bosomed, overweight, overpaid and undertalented, she sets the acting profession back a decade,' said critic David Susskind), Liz still hankered, under Richard's influence, for serious parts in superior dramas. *The Sandpiper* was, unfortunately, one of their most misconceived celluloid couplings. Richard's misgivings about the production were short-lived. Once again, money proved to be the greatest balm for his fears. Liz received an awesome million dollars for her work, Richard three-quarters of her fee. In fact, the audiences should have been paid for watching the film. Despite the glittering credits, this is a truly terrible romantic melodrama in which Taylor, a free-loving beatnik living on the California coast, and Burton, a married Episcopal minister, fall in love after Burton comes into conflict with her over her bastard son's lack of proper schooling. Charles Bronson plays an extremely unlikely sculptor and Eva Marie Saint is Burton's repressed,

Night of the iguana: Richard and Liz contemplate supper

Liz was always in awe of Richard's endless curiosity. He hankered after a life beyond acting

anguished wife. The film is undiluted soap. Richard's screen guilt never gets further than his freckles and Liz's impossibly beautiful Bohemian is an embarrassing travesty of 1960s idealism. However, since this was the first passionate pairing of the two on screen following their respective divorces, audiences flocked to see the couple kissing and fondling. *The Sandpiper* opened at Radio City in New York and broke box-office records despite the reviews.

Things seemed to improve when Richard persuaded Liz to go to Oxford at short notice to star in a student production of *Dr Faustus*. Richard, naturally, played Faustus; Liz, the silent part of Helen of Troy. At the time it seemed as though just about everyone had a play or film to which they considered the Burtons would add a new uncharted dimension. One of those believers was Franco Zeffirelli. In his lusty, bawdy film version of Shakespeare's *The Taming Of The Shrew*, Richard and Liz were actually deployed to uncannily good effect. Burton plays the arrogant ne'er-do-well who marries a rich merchant's impossibly bitchy daughter (Taylor). It's a lesson in humility, entirely at Liz's expense, and the couple believed in the film so much that they sank their own money into it. It worked surprisingly well, but it was yet another film in which the protagonists' private lives seem to be raked up in public.

Although the Burtons frequently described themselves as idle, their work rate was phenomenal. Together, they starred in nine films and graced a further twenty alone. But it's an endless source of speculation as to why the pairing of two such fine actors (and international stars) did not yield more in the way of great art or films. They had fabulous budgets, even more fabulous salaries and worked with some of the greatest directors in the business. But with the rare exception of *Who's Afraid Of Virginia Woolf?* (1966), neither of them seemed able to replicate the intensity and brilliance of former performances. Still, most actors would have died happy if they could have emulated either Richard or Liz's extraordinary performances in Edward Albee's stage play. It was a benchmark movie and a serious art film that changed Hollywood's attitude to bad language on screen forever. Liz was paid $1.1 million by producer Jack Warner for playing the sozzled role of Martha, but she would have undoubtedly appeared in the film for nothing at all. It was Liz who recruited Mike Nichols to direct the movie, although he had never made a film in his life, and it was an utterly inspired choice.

The adaptation of Albee's play provided one of the most discomforting portraits of middle-aged married life ever seen on screen. Burton plays a defeated history professor, George, who is married to Taylor's boorish, alcoholic Martha. When a young couple, George Segal and Sandy Dennis, arrive at their home for a nightcap, George and Martha proceed in a flood of recriminations to describe their dreadful relationship and how they seem to be bound together like two pitbull terriers tied to a stake. At the centre of the plot is a desperate secret held by the couple: a child who may or may not be a figment of Martha's fantasies.

It's an immensely sophisticated film, undeniably brutal in both the language and the demands on the lead players. Liz and Richard more than earned their fees. The film was nominated for thirteen Oscars and won five. Taylor was awarded one (her second), as was Sandy Dennis. The other Oscars went to Richard Sylbert and George James Hopkins for their black-and-white art direction, and to Irene Sharaff for her monochromatic costumes. Burton was nominated, but cruelly pipped at the post by his friend, Paul Scofield, who scored a notable success in *A Man For All Seasons*. Despite Scofield's brilliance, Richard was robbed of an award he richly deserved – he gave a magnificent performance. It's not just a tragedy, but an outright scandal, that he was destined to become the most nominated Oscar performer of all time never to win the award.

How much Burton and Taylor relived their screen roles in *Who's Afraid Of Virginia Woolf?* in their private life will never be truly known. The strain of playing such a dysfunctional, angry and violent couple took its toll on their own marriage. Certainly the swearing and inflammable arguments were no secret in Hollywood or amongst their glittering friends. Liz, having built herself up to a podgy 155 pounds to play Martha, suddenly found that the extra pounds were proving hard to remove.

At first, Elizabeth claimed to enjoy the couple's fights, off-screen and on. But as the 1960s wore on, their drinking became heavier, the arguments more frequent and there were clear signs of wear and tear. Significantly, when Elizabeth first divorced Richard, she reputedly said to her friends that she didn't want to play Martha ever again. To unpractised eyes, the two mega-stars still appeared to be very much in love and obsessed with each other's company. Wherever possible, they worked together and, in many cases, stipulated in their contracts that their individual films be shot in the same city so that they wouldn't have to be apart. No other Hollywood couple, then or since, could claim the same kind of treatment. However, it was increasingly difficult to negotiate the same financial terms as age and familiarity began to erode their combined box-office appeal. Curiously it was Richard who steadily became more in demand than Liz.

Joseph Losey's *Boom!* (1968), based on another Tennessee Williams' play, *The Milk Train Doesn't Stop Here Anymore*, presciently encapsulated their problems. In the film, the millionaire heroine (Taylor), slowly dying in her isolated palace near Sardinia, spends most of her days drinking heavily, popping pills and swearing at servants. Burton, a somewhat mystical figure, stumbles into her life and is promptly used by her as a plaything. He watches her bleeding her life away while acting as friend, lover and even 'saviour'.

Generally regarded as one of the biggest flops in Hollywood history, *Boom!* was intended to boost the couple's sagging credibility, but it inadvertently magnified what many fans began to grumble about: an almost wilful double-act of self-indulgence. Some critics regard it as the perfect film in which to analyse two actors who are capable of brilliance but who choose instead to make complete and utter fools of themselves. This is too harsh. Yes, there is unintentional comedy in the film, but also some originality, albeit mostly due to Noel Coward's brief appearance as a character dubbed the Witch of Capri.

For Liz it was a time to face facts. She looked as if she had finally reached the point of no turning back when in 1969 she went up for the part of Anne Boleyn, second wife to Richard Burton's Henry VIII and mother of Elizabeth I, in *Anne Of The*

Richard and Liz in the swim, and very much in love

Thousand Days. With devastating bluntness, Liz was told that she was too old for the part and it went to a younger and much prettier Canadian actress, Genevieve Bujold, who, to add insult to injury, was Oscar-nominated for the part. Even harder to stomach for poor Liz were the rumours circulating about Richard and his leading lady. Although these were probably unfounded, they didn't prevent a hyper-jealous Liz from turning up on set for all the love scenes. Bujold must have been utterly unnerved by Liz's steaming presence. It's hard enough to fake emotions on set in front of a camera with one of the world's most desirable leading men, and surely impossible when his wife is silently censoring your every move. Genevieve Bujold should have won the statuette for that alone.

Eventually, Richard himself started to look fallible. A wave of poor reviews started to eat away at his his confidence. Worse, his interest in acting as a career was waning and he yearned for the careers that he had never given himself enough time to pursue while chasing Liz and the Holy Grail of glittering screen stardom. Richard was intelligent and talented enough to do other things. His copious diaries reveal a

A buxom Liz in a space age fright wig. Taste never impeded her ability to make a public splash

naturally gifted writer with a wicked sense of humour and a Dickensian eye for social and intellectual detail. Whether his ambitions were ultimately substantial enough to sustain him, it is impossible to tell. In maudlin moments, he professed to certain favoured journalists that he longed to drop the acting and maybe try his hand as a full-time writer, teacher, professor, even journalist. He often talked about going to Oxford to teach but these pipe dreams increasingly seemed to retract in direct proportion to his yearning for them.

The reason for this was almost certainly the enormous strains on the Burtons' marriage. Throughout most of their waking lives, they were now living their lives as though in a goldfish bowl: pestered by the paparazzi and constantly surrounded by a ridiculously large entourage. To be alone together wasn't just hard to arrange; it was impossible. The five children from their previous marriages were always turning up and Liz's ever-expanding collection of pets had turned the house they shared into a small-scale zoo. Travelling was a major military operation and big security teams were regularly needed. Wherever they went, the couple were surrounded by a team of secretaries, hairdressers, henchmen, maids, nannies, animals and hangers-on. They were an exceptionally restless, easily bored pair and spending money was one way not just of staving off the boring masses, but of distracting themselves from the problems within their relationship.

From his diaries, one discovers how much Richard loved and doted on Liz, but also how much he craved for peace from this human and animal menagerie. It seemed an almost impossible dream. The demands on both of them were endless. The difference between the two was that Liz had been in demand since she was 12 years old and although fame was no longer a new thing for Richard, he hadn't equipped himself early enough with the emotional steel to deal with it, and certainly not at this level.

Perhaps the saddest feature of Richard's life is that the very thing he once craved – fame – inexorably wore down his good nature and big heart. However, he was quite willing to live his life (and arguments) in public. Liz was a well-practised, if increasingly cynical, opponent. In 1964 guests at a hotel in Amalfi were amazed to see the Burtons' entire wardrobe fly out of the window and land in the sea. One of Richard's lifelong habits was that he would always make up with Liz by buying her enormously expensive jewellery. Some of these pieces were staggering. The 33-carat Krupp diamond and a Cartier diamond worth over $1 million are legendary pieces in the gem market.

Liz, whose appetite for jewellery was second to none, was happy to accept great mounds of gems. Ever since she was a teenager, the acquisition of baubles had been an outward sign of worth; the giving and receiving of them a substantial token of loyalty and friendship. With the unbelievable amounts of money they earned at the height of their fame, the Burtons freely indulged in spending vast sums on each other, as often as not to make up for the more bloody fall-outs in their marriage. They spent on an unprecedented scale – they could afford to. Between them, they accumulated a staggering $87 million from acting, and spent $65 million maintaining their decadent lifestyle.

Musician Dave Stewart, the creative force behind one of the most lucrative pop music duos this century – The Eurythmics – may have been the first person to highlight the 'paradise syndrome', a condition where people make up illnesses because life is just too perfect for them. The same condition might be diagnosed in Richard Burton and Elizabeth Taylor, although most of the planet laboured under the illusion that life in the liberated hippy 1960s could not be more perfect for two such glittering stars. They were like perpetual lottery winners, but the truth of the matter is that their paradise was full of pitfalls. In his diaries, Burton documents countless incidents of pain and bleeding due to Taylor's uterine problems, haemorrhoids and addictions. In July 1968, at just 36 years of age, Liz underwent a hysterectomy. Richard, who took a room next to hers in the hospital, wrote in his diary: 'I have just spent the two most horrible days of my adult life.' He described Liz as being 'in screaming agony for two days, hallucinating on drugs, sometimes knowing who I was and sometimes not'. When Richard himself went through periodic, self-imposed stretches of abstinence, he would constantly agonize over his wife's own appetite for alcohol and painkillers. In 1969 he described her as being 'astonishingly drunk even as I got to lunch'. It is clear that paradise was in perpetual danger of being lost.

Considering their joint tendency toward self-destructive behaviour and their love of the extravagant highlife, hopes of leading a normal life together receded like an ebbing tide. After so many fat pay cheques, neither of them would dream of stooping to an equity wage. Fame was insistent in its own expectations. Compromises were not tolerated. In short, the pair were becoming harder to employ, and even more expensive to maintain.

Richard felt the need to flaunt the couple's mutual wealth perhaps more than Liz. He wanted the world to know how much he paid for things, boasting to one journalist that he outspent Aristotle Onassis and that being married to Liz cost him $1,000 a minute. The exercise was designed to convince the critics (but most of all himself) of how happy they were. Over a period of ten years the couple purchased

*Wherever they went, whatever they did, Liz and Richard were never
more than a snapshot away from the front pages of the newspapers*

Richard and Liz wilting under the glare of the paparazzi

property in Switzerland, Ireland, Mexico, London, Rome and the Caribbean. $192,000 was spent on a luxury yacht and a further $240,000 on refurbishing it. Apocryphal stories abound. Richard wanted to fly to Nice for lunch so he bought a ten-seater jet for $1 million. And so it went. Together, they began to amass a serious art collection which included works by Monet, Van Gogh, Renoir and Degas, although Richard would be the first to admit that he was more impressed with the price tags than the art the money bought.

Pundits calculated that Elizabeth spent close to $100,000 on clothes each year. That didn't, of course, include the diamond accessories. Those who wanted the couple to work with them knew Liz's weakness only too well. Producers, as well as directors, soon learned that the best way to keep the star sweet on a film set was to present her with jewels. It might seem strange that someone considered so beautiful should need so many ostentatious trinkets, but Liz quite rightly believed that you can never have too much of a good thing. There was an implicit understanding between herself and Richard that as the bigger star, she should naturally be the centre of attention. The wearing of world-famous jewels simply served to underline the fact.

It didn't cut much ice with the *New York Times*. When Burton bought the Cartier diamond at auction, the paper was so outraged by the extravagance that it said: 'In an age of vulgarity marked by such minor matters as war and poverty, it gets harder every day to scale the heights of true vulgarity. But given some loose millions, it can be done – and, worse, admired.' Elizabeth's brilliant reply to the paper was: 'I know I'm vulgar, but would you have it any other way?'

Richard rather naively didn't expect these public demonstrations of wealth to be so isolating. How could it be otherwise? For old friends and family it was almost impossible to comprehend the wealth. These close friends and relatives often had real problems trying to breach the various levels of the duo's entourage and communicate with the two stars themselves. It was difficult for Richard to sound genuinely happy, given the hordes of hacks who followed them with telescopic lenses and bristling microphones. The couple's social circle began to recede to the most exclusive, moneyed groups. Richard and Liz would only venture out at the invitation of Baron and Baroness Guy de Rothschild, Princess Elizabeth of Yugoslavia, and Princess Grace and Prince Rainier of Monaco. Despite being the people's royalty, they had little time for those who didn't have the same drawing power and financial muscle as they did. There were only a privileged few in the world who were not unduly awed by the mystique and financial clout of Richard Burton and Elizabeth Taylor.

Richard's charm could disarm the most snobbish of their new circle, but he was never so at ease as Elizabeth. The Burtons may have been at the top of everyone's A list, but in his black moods Richard had a scary habit of shooting himself in the foot, mostly by drinking too much, then speaking his mind with scathing contempt for those he didn't consider had the wit to share the same airspace. It was frequently a source of acute embarrassment. And although he was usually contrite the next day, it didn't stop him from belching loudly, cutting someone dead and then tottering out, usually the worse for wear. He could rarely stomach the sheer boredom of this hermetic list of ambassadorial parties unless he was tanked up.

Richard, like many ruddy leading men of the time, including Richard Harris, Peter O'Toole and the late Oliver Reed, had always been a hearty, shameless boozer. It's not idle speculation to suggest that he regarded it as an essential part of his personality. Like many great actors before and since, Richard almost certainly succumbed to the potent myth that drink contributed to his machismo and image as a wild and amusing person. Everyone with more than a healthy taste for alcohol feels they are invariably more interesting after a few drinks. The age-old difficulty is knowing exactly where to stop. Richard had a great party piece. His memory was as fabulous as his ability to sink cocktails. He could recite epic speeches, long and twisted poems, and indeed whole plays word-perfect in a state of intoxication that would have left mere mortals clutching the floorboards under the table. His benders were every bit as colourful and long-lived as Olly Reed's. They would invariably be more entertaining, simply because Richard had a warehouse of anecdotes and scripts in his head from which he could draw at will. The problem is that when Richard went bingeing he could be gone for days. Far from easing the stress, the drink actually exacerbated it.

Liz was amazingly tolerant of his boozing for most of their marriage. Indeed rather than preaching at him, or invoking the wrath of the wounded wife, she was often happy to join him. In retrospect, perhaps more than happy. Liz herself could put away formidable quantities of Jack Daniels. Sometimes they drank to ease the pain of various ailments. Liz's are well-documented in this book, but Richard suffered from arthritis, although he always tried to ignore it. But alcohol is the most insidious of crutches.

In an uncomfortable way, the couple's reliance on one another actually depended on their inadequacies. Where moderation was concerned, they both clearly lacked self-discipline. On those increasingly rare occasions when Richard kicked the bottle to salvage his kidneys, Liz would invariably carry on, forever

Liz, Richard and Katherine Burton leaving the Fitzroy Nuffield Nursing Home,
Marylebone, London, where Liz had a partial hysterectomy operation on July 21, 1968

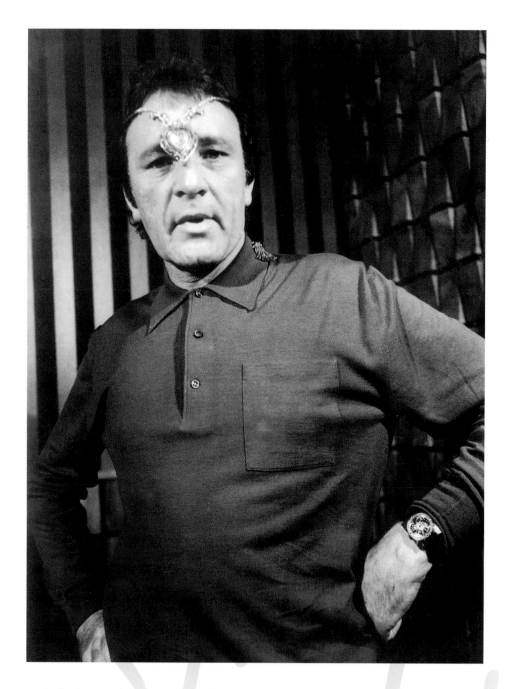

Richard sporting the £380,000 diamond pendant that he gave to Liz on her 40th birthday. What a card

putting temptation his way. It must have been excruciatingly difficult for Richard, who could never find a happy medium between being totally dry and drowning in the stuff. The effect it had on their children – the two Wilding boys, Liza Todd, Richard and Liz's adopted daughter Maria Burton, and Richard's two daughters by Sybil Burton – can only be imagined.

Liz, one suspects, would have loved to have had children by Richard, but following the operation on her womb after the birth of Liza Todd, this was now an impossible dream – and a likely source of pain for someone who had proved herself a doting mother. Liz was, and remains, crazy about her kids. The children always had to be near her and, consequently, they lived a somewhat nomadic life. Lack of continuity in their home life and a stable education affected their studies, in some cases dramatically. At seven, Liza Todd could speak two languages but she was unable to read because she had not been to school. A succession of nannies, governesses and tutors could not recreate the classroom environment endured by most kids. Richard was quite keen to send them to boarding school, which would have been a sensible option under the circumstances. Liza went to Heathfield, a girls' boarding school, and the boys attended Millfield until they were expelled.

It was hardly surprising that it would take the children most of their lives to sort themselves out. The boys fared hardest of all, particularly Michael, the eldest. He became a hippie and rejected his parents' wealthy lifestyle to become part of a Welsh commune. One can understand Richard's apparent fury, just as much as one can understand why Michael opted out of the circus. It had taken Richard a superhuman effort and an enormous amount of luck to dig himself out of the poverty trap. He must have thought Michael's choice to immerse himself in a commune lifestyle – in Wales, of all places – was a rejection of all he had achieved, and therefore a rejection of both Liz and himself. For Michael it must have been utterly liberating, bailing out of the chaotic lifestyle that shackled his mother and his step-father to a non-stop merry-go-round of high living. After a failed first marriage, Michael eventually became an actor in California. Christopher Wilding's first marriage to one of the Gettys – Aileen – was also doomed to fail. Liza made the most successful transition into adulthood, marrying her long-standing artist boyfriend and becoming an equestrian sculptress. Maria, who is perhaps closest to Liz, is a housewife in Manhattan. Considering the strangeness of their upbringing and the wealth with which the children were surrounded, they have turned out remarkably well-adjusted.

By the end of the 1960s, cracks in the Burton marriage were beginning to turn into chasms. Richard's dry periods of self-control were getting rarer. His venom was growing more poisonous and his levels of tolerance were dropping through the bottom of his glass. There were small but significant family tragedies. His brother, Ivor, ever loyal to Richard despite Richard's painful divorce from Sybil, fell over a loose grill when he tried to gain entrance to Richard's hideaway house in Celigny, Switzerland, and became paralysed from the neck down. Richard was horrified, needlessly quick to blame himself and, as ever in times of stress, he took familiar recourse to the bottle.

For the next decade the couple were plagued with minor and major ailments: broken fingers, bad backs and Liz's alarming tendency to be accident-prone. She severed an artery on her left forearm while on holiday in Yugoslavia in 1973. In the same year, she was hospitalized in Los Angeles with a cyst that wouldn't stop bleeding. While shooting *The Blue Bird* in Leningrad in 1975, she suffered amoebic dysentery. Liz's extraordinary capacity for painkillers, combined with the couple's long-term battle with alcoholism, would prove crucial factors in the eventual breakdown of their marriage.

At the beginning of the 1970s, however, Elizabeth was having to come to terms with the fact that her box-office appeal was seriously waning. *The Only Game In Town*, in which she starred with Warren Beatty, was not a commercial success. In fact, it was one of the most expensive flops in Fox's history. Although nowhere near the scale of *Cleopatra* in terms of money staked, it was nevertheless a telling dent in her *œuvre*. Liz insisted that it should be filmed in Paris because Burton was there, making a movie called *Staircase* with Rex Harrison. Fox spent a fortune building Las Vegas sets at the Studios de Boulogne. The production cost about three times as much to make in Paris as it would have cost if they had shot it in Nevada and instead brought Richard and Rex over and paid for them to shoot *Staircase* in the States. Added to that was the $2 million paid to the stars. It's easy to see how the bills began to mount, and it's even easier to spot who was to blame.

Frank Sinatra was originally chosen to play the male lead instead of Warren Beatty, but when Liz fell ill and the production was temporarily derailed, Frank bowed out. After turning down *Butch Cassidy And The Sundance Kid*, Beatty took the lead. George Stevens, who had previously directed Liz in *Giant* and *A Place In The Sun*, had returned to shoot *The Only Game In Town* after a gap of five years. He himself was on the rebound from lukewarm reviews of his last film, *The Greatest Story Ever Told*. Shooting in France took eighty days and it still wasn't enough. The company spent ten more days in Las Vegas, including location photography under Bob Swink. Despite all the time and effort involved, the plot can be summed up in just a few

1971: Liz and Richard slope through Heathrow airport after visiting Liz's granddaughter. Richard seems rather less than enamoured of Liz's cocktail outfit

*1975: Liz meets her oldest son, Christopher Wilding, for the first time in six years. Chris had opted out of
the lifestyle of the superstar child by going AWOL in Wales. Richard was less than impressed*

words: Liz plays a tired Vegas showgirl who has been having an affair with married
swinger Charles Braswell, a wealthy San Franciscan businessman. He pays her rent
and buys her a fabulous wardrobe of clothes. Beatty is a gambling junkie, who plays
the piano for Hank Henry to pay off money he owes around town. Beatty moves in
with Taylor, the inevitable happens and they fall in love. A lot of the dialogue
sparkles, but it's basically a dressed-up melodrama. In 1970 the picture opened in Las
Vegas and audiences queued up to leave. It was a major waste of an estimated budget
of $11 million. The investors recouped $2 million and Fox executives were left
chewing their hats.

Suddenly, there were no more million-dollar offers rolling in for Liz. For once,
she had priced herself out of the very market she had single-handedly created.
Richard was still working away furiously. It was as if he was trying to make as much
money as possible from his exalted status before it disappeared. However, his
box-office appeal was also drooping. Between 1970 and 1971 he filmed five flops in
a row: *Villain, Under Milk Wood, Hammersmith Is Out, The Battle of Satjesha* and

The Assassination of Trotsky. For someone who spent his life aching and arguing for quality, this must have hurt very badly indeed.

Despite the run of bad luck, the reviews themselves smack of sour grapes. In actual fact these films are classics of their kind. Peter Ustinov's *Hammersmith Is Out* is a collector's item. It's a Burton-Taylor vehicle and another variation on the Faust legend, but it's also an endearingly mad caper. Ustinov's film features a mental patient (Burton) promising wealth and power to a male nurse (Beau Bridges) in return for his help in escaping from the hospital. Along with a waitress (Taylor), they set out on a string of antisocial money-making schemes. Before long, Bridges has the power and wealth promised him, but Burton and Taylor conspire to cut him out of the picture. The production looks a little bloated, but Richard's blank and inscrutable Mephistopheles figure and Liz's screeching, drawling waitress are unforgettable cinematic gargoyles.

In such a fraught and close relationship off-screen, the two actors started cannibalizing their own abilities and energies. Liz's constant demands were taking their toll on Richard's energy. He looked distinctly weary, even on film, and prone to fits of melancholy. In his few married years to Liz, he had achieved everything that he had ever have possibly hoped for – fame, money, power and a beautiful wife – only to find that it didn't bring him the kind of personal fulfilment and happiness one half expects from silver-lined dreams. Awards may be one of fame's great hangovers, but Richard hankered after one, or several, to keep on an even keel with his wife. An Oscar would have been no less than he deserved; a knighthood would have entirely fitting; a Chair at Oxford University would have been a dream too far. The CBE that he accepted was always going to be too little. For such a unique talent, he never, in short, got what he really deserved.

Burton's diaries reveal how he was still deeply in love with and fascinated by Elizabeth Taylor, almost embarrassingly so. But there was bound to be a crunch at some point and it came about in 1972 when Richard and Liz were in Hungary, where he was filming *Bluebeard*. Richard presented the £380,000 Shah Jehan yellow diamond to Liz as her fortieth birthday present and threw a typically glittering party. He was having a dry spell and all seemed well. Less than a month later, however, his brother Ivor died. Domestic mayhem ensued. Richard flipped completely and went on a drinking and womanizing binge that seemed impossible for Liz to halt. She was miserable enough to fly to Rome to have dinner with Aristotle Onassis (by this time Onassis was having his own marital difficulties with Jackie). It was almost a calculated manoeuvre to make Richard jealous. To all intents and purposes he was beyond caring. It now seemed only a matter of time before the Burtons parted: enough time for them to make their last film together in Munich, the aptly named and pretty terrible TV movie, *Divorce His, Divorce Hers*.

Never a couple to do things quietly, the Burtons' break-up was as overblown and newsworthy as their initial romance had been. Taylor announced the separation to the world. She said that she hoped the parting would ultimately bring them closer together and asked people to 'Wish us well during this difficult time. Pray for us.' To this, Burton replied (not to Taylor, but to Nigel Dempster of the *Daily Mail*): 'You can't keep clapping a couple of sticks together without expecting them to blow up.' He ended his insight with the statement: 'There is no question of our love and devotion to each other. I don't even consider that Elizabeth and I are separated.'

The world waited for a reconciliation and, sure enough, when Burton announced that he had given up drinking, Taylor flew back to be by his side. Ironically, she had been in Rome, where she was filming a TV movie, *The Driver's Seat*. Nine days later, it was all over. Richard announced to the press that divorce was the only option: '… if two people are absolutely sick of each other, or the sight of one another bores them.' Liz was devastated but, true to form, she could not leave one man without having another waiting in the wings. Her fear was that Richard might find and – more importantly – declare a partner publicly before she did. She promptly began a relationship with Henry Wynberg, a Beverly Hills playboy whom she had recently met. Although he is said to have been a good lover, the Dutch used-car salesman, though charming, proved something of a rogue. He was later convicted of fraud, but this did not seem to deter an embattled Liz.

Wynberg came from a working-class family and his first job had been as a luggage boy in the foyer of Amsterdam's Krasnapolsky Hotel. When he was only 16, he set sail for America and lived the life of a thrusting opportunist (complete with a couple of marriages) until he encountered Liz, who was on the rebound from Richard. In many respects, Wynberg represented a dry run for Liz's later husband, Larry Fortensky. As Wynberg himself admitted, he was just a distraction for Liz. In a newspaper article he declared that her mind was always elsewhere: 'Burton had bought her heart and he owned the freehold.' Hearing of Burton's decision to divorce Taylor, Wynberg tracked her down to Rome and made a concerted play for her. It was only half successful. Says Wynberg: 'Liz was forever rushing thousands of miles to throw him out and begin again.' She was grieving, probably in a way that she had never grieved before or since. Burton was everything that a woman could ever want, but he was still Burton, a human being, with all his faults. The tragedy is that the

Liza Todd and Liz Taylor: Mike Todd's daughter inherited her mother's spectacular eyes

End of the affair: Richard and Liz on a train to nowhere

couple, as Wynberg and the rest of the world saw it, were never able to accept one another as the people they truly were.

There was one more public reconciliation before the divorce papers were signed. Elizabeth had a suspected malignant tumour that later proved to be benign and by now Richard was drinking so seriously that he ended up in hospital because of it. On 26 June 1974, their first divorce came through. For Liz and Richard fans it was an outright catastrophe. For the next eighteen months the two took other partners. Richard, although the mind boggles, became engaged to Princess Elizabeth of Yugoslavia (Liz had considered her to be a great friend). Liz had a mad fling with Wynberg, who accompanied her to Russia when she filmed *Bluebird*. Later, he would be inducted as a major player and partner in her 'Passion' perfume business.

For all the melodramatic behaviour, Richard and Liz were constantly on the phone to each other, and all the more so after his engagement to Princess Elizabeth of Yugoslavia was called off. The pristine Princess was less than amused at Richard's romantic dalliance with a *Playboy* centrefold model. By August 1975, the couple were missing each other's bad habits too much and were reconciled. Being out of each other's orbit was proving a far harder job than sharing the same air. Richard found himself on his knees once more asking Liz to marry him. On 10 October 1975, they went through Liz's most surreal wedding ceremony, which took place on the banks of the river in the Chobe Game Reserve in Botswana. For a few months before the wedding, Liz lived in a happy cloud of wishful thinking that their relationship would be as good as it had once been in the past. Unfortunately, on the morning of the wedding, Richard took his first drink in weeks and he was drunk by 8 a.m. 'Sturm has remarried Drang,' wrote the *Boston Globe*, 'and all is right with the world'. Cruel, sure, but also spot on.

Immediately, the couple's old problems resurfaced with a vengeance. Richard was struck down with malaria and he was fighting a losing, and ever darker, battle against drink. Liz went back into hospital with serious neck and back pains. She needed constant pampering, perhaps the kind she couldn't get in a relationship, but Richard was increasingly loath to give it. When they managed to spend some time together, the two fought constantly, but whenever Richard wanted some peace and quiet on his own, Liz was bereft without him. The crunch came at Christmas in Gstaad. In the most banal of circumstances, Richard went skiing to get away from the endless demands of his wife and spotted a very tall and beautiful blonde British model, Susie Hunt. The 27-year-old, recently separated from racing driver James Hunt, soon became his lover.

Liz was duly mortified, as were legions of motor racing fans, and Liz sensed that this time it was serious. When Richard left for New York, where he was to star in Peter Shaffer's *Equus*, his first stage play since *Hamlet*, it was Susie, and not Elizabeth, who accompanied him. Elizabeth was desperate. She could never bear to be alone – least of all publicly alone – and she immediately began a seven-week, tense affair with a 37-year-old advertising executive, Peter Darmanian, whom she met at a club. Darmanian recalled later how they were never apart and often stayed in bed until two in the afternoon and only got dressed for dinner. But these bedroom stunt-men got short shrift from Liz. They had no real idea what they were dealing with. Darmanian was swiftly and resoundingly dismissed when Richard asked Liz to meet him in New York.

The table talk was chilly. Richard asked Liz for a divorce as he intended to marry Susie Hunt. An inconsolable Elizabeth cancelled her forty-fourth birthday party and flew back to California to be in the arms of Henry Wynberg. As a couple, the Burtons had finally reached the limits of their endurance. Several months later when she realized that there was no hope of reconciliation, Elizabeth granted Richard a divorce and she quickly moved on, the instinct being to bury as quickly as possible the feelings for the only man she had ever really loved since Mike Todd. But this was to be no ordinary parting. Liz always held a torch for Richard. How could she not? In the hermetic glass bowls in which they both moved, they could hardly avoid each other forever.

Henry Wynberg loomed out of the shadows to escort Liz

Liz and Richard would never truly get over each other

But in the end, the constant attention and prying contributed to their final split

CHAPTER V

THE ROAD TO OBLIVION

Regrettably, there came a point in Elizabeth's career when the absurd extremes of her life began to bemuse even her most devoted fans. In the disco-mad, flared-trousered jungle of the 1970s, the sparkle was coming off Liz's glittering superstardom. Her second divorce from Richard Burton suddenly looked like the start of a very long downhill slope. Liz needed to put the brakes on. She needed to try to find a new direction for her life, perhaps even kick-start her stalled career. She needed, in short, a massive injection of confidence.

In 1976, Liz was invited to a series of fund-raising benefits and Bicentennial receptions in Washington. She was endlessly photographed with senators, dancers (including Mikhail Baryshnikov), chic designers and squads of political diplomats, most notably the dashing Iranian ambassador, Ardeshir Zahedi. Zahedi made no secret of his attempts to woo her to the Iranian cause. She was flattered by the attention, and the seed of a new deserving cause was sown in Liz's imagination. The world of politics seemed to beckon. Given the diplomatic problems that would develop between the US and Tehran under Ronald Reagan and the Ayatollah Khomeni, it seems rather comical now that Liz tried to highlight shared interests between the US and Iran by leading a prestigious party to the Iranian capital to live it up. Washington bigwigs were less than impressed with this self-styled form of diplomacy, but it gave Liz a taste for politics and campaigning that she would never lose.

On the personal front, it was one of those rare, dangerous times in Liz's life when she was footloose but suffering from figure problems. To stave off the post-Burton

All wrapped up and nowhere to go: Liz started getting the chills about the endless public scrutiny of her private life

Hooking up with her seventh husband and Republican wannabe, John Warner

blues, she had been turning to her ample fridge rather more frequently than she did to her friends. Her weight ballooned. The exotic cocktail of alcoholic drinks and powerful tranquillizers didn't help.

Liz, however, was still a desirable commodity. One heavily smitten escort was John William Warner Junior, a six-foot patrician dandy with a blinkered ambition to make it very big in politics. Warner, five years older than Liz, was an out-and-out Virginian Republican. He had all the ingredients of the political right stuff. Warner had served in World War II and with the Marines in Korea. He was from a staunch middle-class family. They were not particularly rich, but they were stable and financially comfortable enough to support him through law school and pave the way for a position as an assistant US attorney in Washington.

Warner had already married well, and divorced even better. His ex-wife, Catherine Mellon, came from one of the richest families in America. If the truth be told, it was Catherine who opened doors and eased John's way into influential positions first as Secretary of the Navy, and then as director of the American Revolution Bicentennial Administration. The couple split, ostensibly because John wanted a woman who would be happy to look good on his arm in the Senate and Catherine, who had spent a lifetime doing much the same with her influential family, couldn't stand the thought of more role-playing. John's divorce settlement, over $7.5 million, gave him ample scope to indulge his rather tweedy, pipe-smoking, ranch-owning image. By all accounts, he was utterly dull and prone to making social blunders, but alluring and sexy enough for Liz to sink her teeth into.

At 44, Liz was no longer on the end of gold-encrusted movie offers and Warner represented the change of direction she hankered after. The idyllic country package that came with him attracted her and the couple were duly married on 4 December 1976. The only interruption to Warner's smooth acquisition was Liz's contractual obligation to appear in the movie version of Stephen Sondheim's *A Little Night Music* and a walk-on cameo in the TV film, *Victory At Entebbe*.

Liz's heart was clearly not in the uninspired screen version of Sondheim's tart musical revue, lifted from Ingmar Bergman's film, *Smiles of A Summer Night*. *A Little Night Music* is an elaborate musical homage that centres on a turn-of-the-century country house party at which virginities are lost, adulteries floated and true love wins through. Harold Prince's film version is devoid of startling or original filmic ideas but it did give Liz her least ridiculous part in a decade and it boasts generally decent performances all round. Of course, you wouldn't expect any less with Diana Rigg, Lesley-Anne Down and Hermione Gingold in the cast.

To John Warner's delight, Elizabeth brought out the crowds whenever he spoke in public, which was often. He had set his sights on a seat at the Senate and launched Liz at student unions, fund-raisers and any political event where he thought she might curry favour. Liz, perhaps still burning with a new-found sense of political fervour, was astonishingly acquiescent. She may not have been the ideal Virginian country farmer's wife, but when there were hands to press and embarrassing questions to answer, Liz came up trumps. She was a natural audience winner, but after a lifetime avoiding the publicity she now so openly courted on John's behalf, Liz didn't suffer these inquisitions – and the sacrifices they entailed – at all lightly.

Little by little, the new role of Republican wife began to gnaw away at Liz's sense of self-esteem. Playing second fiddle was not in her natural repertoire. The American Senate campaign trail is one of the toughest electioneering circuits in the world. Liz's drinking, which occurred so often when she was angry and desperate with Richard, was now a means of anaesthetizing herself from the exhausting, selfless business of winning her husband a seat.

Once again, films provided a retreat of sorts from the campaign grind. Liz performed another cameo in a political thriller called *Winter Kills*. She didn't have a single line to utter in the film, but it was a witty and intelligent piece that thinly satirized and probed the death of the late great J F Kennedy. However, everyone who saw the limited release could see the inches piling on her. The rest of 1977 was a blizzard of campaign speeches, baby-kissing and gruesome rallies. Somehow Liz kept her sanity, but she did lose her taste for her husband's career.

By the time she returned to Hollywood to shoot *Return Engagement* (aka *Repeat Performance*) in the summer of 1978, improbably cast as an ancient history professor who falls chastely in love with a young student, Liz was thoroughly fed up. According to a reporter on the scene, she relayed that: 'People are looking for wrinkles and pimples, and I don't disappoint them. They want to see if my eyes are really violet, or bloodshot, or both. Once they check me out, they can go home and say: "I saw Liz Taylor and you know what? She ain't so hot!" And you know what? They're right. She ain't.'

All that suffering seemed to be for nothing. Warner narrowly lost the election to the Republican nomination to the Senate that he was so desperate to earn. His career looked as if it might crawl down a cul-de-sac. But the sudden death of Richard Obenshain (the winning opponent) on 11 August 1978 dramatically cleared the way for him to have a priceless second attempt at the Senate. He spent $1.2 million and put Liz on a killer schedule of appointments. The gargantuan effort paid off in three

Liz flirting with the fans and wearing cuffs most people would give their eye teeth for

The Houses of Hollywood and Windsor: Elizabeth Taylor and Princess Diana meeting after a performance of The Little Foxes. *Diana was pregnant with Prince William*

intense months. On 7 November 1978, Warner won the Virginia seat by the skin of his teeth. Two weeks earlier Liz had choked on a chicken bone at a political buffet and was hospitalized. When she got up on the platform to congratulate her husband, the sincerity must have stuck in her throat.

Liz had more than repaid her half of the marriage ticket: she won Warner his seat to the detriment of her health, mental as much as physical. Perhaps the greatest irony is that she didn't even agree with his politics. Liz wasn't a Republican at heart; she wasn't even an American citizen. Legally Switzerland was her country of nationality and her natural inclinations were towards liberalism. It was hardly surprising that many of Warner's conservative constituency were dubious about a star with Liz's chequered past standing up as their elected symbol of propriety. There was a general unease about the way in which Warner had used her. The Republican ranks were uncomfortable too about Warner's ability to play a major part in government. While her husband set about trying to justify his newly won place in the Senate, Liz was cast adrift.

For Liz, the early months of 1979 were spent in limbo. She barely saw her husband. There were more accidents as she stumbled about, numb with drink, in search of the purpose that she had left behind in the studios and Warner's ballot box. She expanded at a rate of knots. Her rings no longer fitted her plump fingers and she sold a 69.42 carat Cartier diamond – a gift from Richard Burton – for $3 million.

At times, Liz showed remarkable resilience. She checked into a Florida spa and lost 25 pounds. Another time, she had her mouth rewired with oral surgery. But as far as her public were concerned, her greatest increasingly one-sided battle was with the bulge. The necessity of having to put on a public show of contentment as a politician's wife was extremely difficult for her. The military-minded Warner was not schooled in the gentle arts of confidence building and appeared to treat her as one of his chattels. Liz's loneliness was compounded by the death of Michael Wilding on 8 July 1979. He had a wretched end, brought on by alcohol and the deaths of his third and fourth wives, Susan Nell and Margaret Leighton. When he died, his career was largely forgotten and the children were grown-up and leading their own lives.

By 1980, Liz's weight had gone back to over 180 pounds and she became a much abused object of ridicule. The famously cynical exposé of tinseltown, *Hollywood Babylon*, had just been re-issued with a gruesome picture of her on the cover. She was mercilessly sent up at every opportunity, most notably by the sharp-tongued comedienne, Joan Rivers: 'Elizabeth Taylor went to Sea World, saw Shamu [the killer whale] and asked "Does he come with fries?"' To combat the humiliation, she continued to pop tranquillizers, while taking public swipes at her husband. The marriage charade couldn't last.

An offer of work in England from director Guy Hamilton on the Agatha Christie thriller, *The Mirror Crack'd*, provided a badly-needed escape route. It was Liz's first speaking role in almost four years. Anyone who recalls Margaret Rutherford's version of Agatha Christie's Miss Marple may be disappointed with Angela Lansbury's portrayal of the redoubtable spinster detective, but Liz fitted in perfectly with the sly dialogue, cagey characters and unexpected twists of plot. Most enjoyably, the thriller brought Liz and Rock Hudson back into frame in their first reunion since *Giant*. The relief of working with old friends was reciprocated in the performances.

Liz is excellent in a role that she was actually living at the time. She plays a glamorous, ageing actress hell-bent on making a comeback. The past, however, comes back to haunt her. Ghoulishly, her character relives a tragedy that befell the actress Gene Tierney. After Tierney contracted German measles during pregnancy, her first daughter was born retarded. In the film, the person suspected of having caused the tragedy now lives in the small hamlet where Liz, under Tony Curtis' wing, has been persuaded to star in a film version of *Mary, Queen Of Scots*. The shapely Kim Novak turns up to share top billing and there are loaded sparks as the two heavyweights tear strips off each other while bodies mysteriously heap up around them. It's a fabulous piece of hokum. 'I'm so glad to see you've kept your figure,' miaows Novak, 'and added so much to it.' Such closeness to the truth gives this enjoyable thriller a giddy, surreal twist.

Liz's appetite for film work was revitalized by this comeback, even if the juiciest parts were no longer flowing in her direction. Being at home with John Warner was an increasingly joyless existence, but she was still possessed of her marbles. When the producer Zev Bufman offered her a chance to redeem the role of Martha in a Broadway revival of *Who's Afraid Of Virginia Woolf?*, Liz had the good sense to decline the offer. Bufman had the bizarre idea of casting her opposite Burt Reynolds. Thankfully, the idea was shelved. However, Bufman was not to be denied his opportunity to produce Liz. The project was changed to a production of Lillian Hellman's *The Little Foxes*, for which Bufman promised to pay Liz a record stage fee of more than $50,000 a week. It was an incredibly bold step for Liz, considering the tendency of the press to caricature almost everything she touched. The production not only proved to be a surprising and resounding success, it also gave her enough confidence to start levering John Warner out of her life. Again, she felt an instant identity with her character, Regina, a woman who is driven by greed and men to commit a murder. All the anger at those tedious days on the road with Warner came tumbling out in a blistering performance. Not that the reviews would have mattered a jot: the run sold out before it opened.

To celebrate, Liz bought Frank Sinatra's $2 million mansion in Bel-Air, which he had shared with his first wife, and announced that Mr and Mrs John Warner were separating. By all accounts, it was an excuse to party. Liz, swallowing her grudges against Richard, went skiing with the Burtons, the Edwards (Blake and Julie Andrews) and the Geros (Mark and Liza Minnelli). In fact, the celebrations didn't look as if they would ever let up. By the time she staggered to her fiftieth birthday party in London in February 1982, she was in some considerable mess. Even Richard was shocked at her disintegration. Anne Edwards, quoting Liz, reported in *Ladies Home Journal*, March 1986: 'I reached a point where I would take one or two Percodan

Champagne Liz. She always got into fabulous shape for film parts, no matter how small

They were made for each other even though history begs to differ

mixed with booze before I could go out in the evening and face people. I thought it would help me because that combination would make me kind of talkative. I felt I was being charming. I was probably boring as hell, but it gave me false courage. During the course of an evening – like every four hours – I'd take another two Percodan. And of course, I had hollow legs. I could drink anybody under the table and never get drunk. My capacity to consume was terrifying. I didn't even realize that I was an alcoholic.'

If the drinking was debilitating, the drug taking was positively scary. Daniel Spoto notes in his excellent biography, *Elizabeth Taylor* (Little, Brown and Company, 1996), that apart from her dependence on Jack Daniels, between 1980–85 Liz was issued with more than a thousand prescriptions for twenty-eight different sleeping pills, tranquillizers and narcotics (including Demerol and Valium) by three Californian doctors who were later reprimanded by a medical board. Her problem had actually reached the point where the Los Angeles District Attorney's office had to decide whether or not to press charges for malpractice. In the end, it decided not to.

When Bufman's production of *The Little Foxes* opened for a brief sell-out run in London, nearly a year after it opened on Broadway, Liz's performance was unrecognizable. The British critics mauled the show, but the drubbing was rapidly forgotten when it was suddenly announced that Liz was going to star in another Bufman production of Noel Coward's *Private Lives* with Richard Burton. The press went haywire. Could this be the opportunity for a third marital reunion? The news launched a million dinner party debates the world over – the stage coupling of the two most famous stars of their generation could only be a sure-fire winner. With the added spice that there might be a third mighty romance between them, tickets would be as keenly fought over as bars of gold.

As if to stifle the rumours, Liz acquired a new escort. The quiet and respectable Mexican businessman, Victor Luna, had, in better days, been financial adviser to Liz and Richard during their many property negotiations. Fifty-five years old and the father of four daughters, Luna was the most unlikely partner Liz had stepped out with in some years. Still keen to prove that she had an ambassadorial role to play, in 1983 Liz and Victor departed for a self-styled diplomatic mission to the war-torn Middle East which in hindsight seems as preposterous as it was then grandiose. Liz announced rather pompously that she was going to meet Prime Minister Menachem Begin and President Amin Gemayel to try and achieve peace between Israel and Lebanon. A furious State Department hurried to dismiss claims that they had anything to do with it. The episode was a potentially hazardous piece of meddling which rapidly dissolved into a bizarre fiasco. Liz made some banal claims that love and understanding will conquer all, threw a few presents at bemused children in the Tel Aviv Hilton and departed as haphazardly as she had come. The point of it all remains mysterious.

What interested the newspapers more, however, was the news that Richard had divorced Susie Hunt in Haiti, just days before he was scheduled to go into rehearsals with Liz for Noel Coward's *Private Lives* in March 1983. As Richard notes in his diaries, the rehearsals were disastrous. An addled Liz would turn up half-cut with her memory shot to pieces. Neither of them seemed to take on board the ludicrous irony of the play, in which a divorced couple pick over the wreckage of their subsequent marriages. Perhaps they thought that it was they themselves who were doing the exploiting at the box office.

The final *coup de grace* in the long saga between the couple was played out in the Broadway opening. As Sheridan Morley wittily put it: '*Private Lives* opened in Boston on 7 April to some of the worst reviews since the musical *Pearl Harbor*'.

The production limped into New York in May, with a new director, and barely made it through the summer. Like Peter O'Toole's infamous *Macbeth* at the National Theatre, people came to gawp in amazement. More charitable spectators came to collect a piece of history that never looked like being repeated. Still others came to scorn. 'Coward's brittle farce was almost unrecognizable,' noted Sheridan. 'Richard seemed to sleepwalk through it, while Liz spent most of the time trying to remember what she was supposed to be saying next.'

Few reports actually cared about the play. During one of Liz's by now obligatory illnesses, which ranged from bronchitis to nervous exhaustion, Richard took the opportunity to fly off to Las Vegas and marry his last wife, Sally Hay. It must have hurt Liz deeply. Days later, she announced her engagement to Victor Luna. In eight weeks Liz missed some thirty performances, which was to cost the insurers somewhere in the region of half a million dollars. Despite insurance claims of half a million dollars upwards due to her non-appearances, both Liz and Richard made a small fortune from *Private Lives*.

In November 1983, after a brief Los Angeles run of *Private Lives*, Liz's health had reached, as Spoto calls it, a 'critical mass'. Her body could no longer handle the pills and bourbon. She had reached an all-time low. Hospitalized by an abdominal pain, her old friend Roddy McDowall visited her, together with distraught members of her family. On 5 December she checked herself into the Betty Ford Clinic, in Rancho Mirage near Palm Springs, for seven weeks to detox, straighten out her life and try to reinvent herself before she managed to kill herself.

The clinic was based on short, sharp shock treatment. For the first time in her life, Liz was forced to share a room with another woman. She was restricted to only one phone call a day and had to clean toilets, among other chores around the Clinic. For the first time in her adult life, she was under orders to make her own bed. There was also compulsory group therapy to attend. It was a terrifying regime, but one designed to make inhabitants of the Clinic realise just how much work they had to do – and do themselves. It was a humbling and, initially at least, humiliating experience for her. But she emerged 11 pounds lighter and in the best shape she had been in for a decade. As the first major celebrity to go into the Betty Ford Clinic, Liz single-handedly paved the way for stars such as Mary Tyler Moore, Johnny Cash, Tony Curtis, Peter Lawford, Liza Minnelli, Andy Gibb and Don Johnson. Nowadays few people bat an eye when it's announced that a star retreats to a clinic – it's an acceptable practice. But fifteen years ago it took guts for a star of Liz's stature to admit the need for such seemingly drastic measures. The experience affected her

Liz and Liza Minnelli: the closest Liz ever got to cloning

enough to inspire her to keep a diary about it and then subsequently to write her book, *Elizabeth Takes Off*. 'Fame,' she wrote, 'is schizophrenic. You become somebody else. You're not yourself, but a character you portray.'

After a romantic holiday with her fiancé Victor Luna, Liz played another ageing actress in the TV series, *Hotel*, opposite Roddy McDowall. However, the affair with Luna was not destined to last. Luna could never replace Richard in Liz's affections. On 4 August 1984, Richard Burton suffered a cerebral haemorrhage and a massive stroke while alone in bed. He was rushed to Geneva, but died some hours later. He was 58 years old. The one thing Liz never gambled on was losing Richard in person. She was horrified and went into shock. It signalled the end of an era. For better or worse, Liz Taylor had outlived her fifth and sixth husband but, in many respects, Richard Burton will always be her first and last.

Renewed belief in herself, inspired by the Betty Ford Clinic, probably saved Liz from a dramatic relapse. Her last trip to see Burton's grave in Switzerland (ironically,

Liz Taylor and George Hamilton. He was the ideal escort to
glitzy openings and was mooted as one of Liz's many lovers

his body couldn't be brought back to Britain for tax reasons) was a grim reminder of
how bereft of news the paparazzi had become. Despite arriving before the dawn on
14 August, Liz was hounded by photographers with flashbulbs. She once
memorably described the press as cockroaches: 'Totally amoral and totally fearless.
They're a degenerate group.' That day they certainly lived up to her description.

Liz flew to Wales to console Richard's family, wearing the famous Krupp
diamond that he had given her. Back in New York, she began seeing Dennis Stein,
one-time escort of Joan Collins and a businessman who had made a fortune out of a
designer jeans business. One unexpected but welcome feature of the death of
Richard Burton was a reassessment of Liz and Richard's life's work by audiences and
critics. People began to wake up to the fact that Liz's fifty-four films amounted to a
startling comprehensive history of post-war movie-making. After the 1987 Cannes
Film Festival, the President of France, François Mitterrand, awarded her the ribbon
of the Legion d'Honneur.

However, despite the welcome interest in her past career, Liz only attracted a lot
of minor TV roles, including cameos in soaps such as *General Hospital*, and few truly
major movie roles. After playing one of her first great enemies (the gossip columnist
Louella Parsons in tandem with Jane Alexander's equally poisonous gossip hack

Hedda Hopper in a mischievous biopic called *Malice In Wonderland*), Liz worked for a day (and $100,000) in a civil war mini-series, *North And South*. The cash eased the fact that she had to spend a week in the Santa Monica Medical Centre undergoing treatment for back and neck injuries incurred by the 50-pound period dress she had to wear. This was followed by a television drama, *There Must Be A Pony*, in which she is cast yet again (opposite Robert Wagner) as a screen diva attempting a comeback after mental illness. Liz put in a good performance, but it was becoming difficult to differentiate between type-casting and real life.

As her 55th birthday loomed in 1987, Liz started to look for opportunities outside the acting world. Given the 1980s vogue for celebrity scents, it was not surprising that she should license out her name to a perfume company for a huge fee. Sophia Loren had done much the same in 1980, Joan Collins would soon launch her own brand, 'Spectacular', and Cher marketed 'Uninhibited' in 1998. Others would follow, including Candice Bergen, Catherine Deneuve and Mikhail Baryshnikov. Shrewdly backed by a $10 million promotional campaign, Elizabeth Taylor's 'Passion' became the fourth biggest-selling fragrance in America and made her one of the richest women in the world. For someone who had never run a business before, she had an extraordinarily sharp business mind. She marketed her scents brilliantly. And, for the first time in years, she was in terrific shape. By her birthday she was able to flaunt a 22-inch waist and an 8 1/2-stone figure.

The 500 journalists who turned up for the launch of 'Passion' were rather more interested in whether or not she would marry George Hamilton, who had been squiring Liz, on- and off-screen, for the best part of a year. The couple were recruited to Liz's first western, *Poker Alice*, another TV film where she plays a well-born lady who wins a brothel from Hamilton's gambling slicker. An extraordinary $100,000 was set aside in the budget to provide daily gifts to Liz. As much thought was given to delivering these offerings in ways that would amuse her as was paid to the writing of the script itself. Gift-wrapped 'surprises' arrived by stagecoaches, magicians, bandits and stuntmen. The purpose was as much to make sure Liz turned up every day for the three weeks of shooting, as it was a mark of respect. 'Liz is a child,' remarked Hamilton.

Child or not, she continued to flirt with other escorts including Malcolm Forbes, the fabulously wealthy tycoon and publisher of *Forbes* magazine. Liz began slipping back into her old ways. Franco Zeffirelli persuaded her to fly to Rome during the summer of 1987 to shoot *Young Toscanini*, a story about the composer's wild relationship with a Russian soprano during his tour of Brazil. Doomed by its own

Liz arriving at a reception hosted by Prince and Princess Michael of Kent in 1989

portentous artifice, the movie toured a couple of festivals before being shelved. The stress of the perfume and book promotions inevitably took its toll on Liz. Lack of real work – good, solid film parts, which had been her salvation in the past – was a crucial factor. Even more painfully, she suffered a compression fracture of the third lumbar vertebra in the summer of 1988 and became dependent on painkillers yet again. That, combined with the bottle and the chocolates, proved to be a recipe for disaster.

By autumn 1988 Liz was once again staring into an abyss. On 25 October, she checked into the Betty Ford Clinic for another seven-week stint. It can only have been harder for her the second time around. She duly dried out, but managed to put on more weight, apparently by sneaking takeaways past the clinic's security. Film work dried up to the point where her only notable contribution in 1989 was as Tennessee Williams' ravaged movie star in a TV version of *Sweet Bird Of Youth*. It's a commendable small-screen offering. Mark Harmon plays the hunky youth who is used by a vampirish diva (played by Liz) to prolong her hollow sense of attractiveness. As ever with Liz, events on screen spookily shadowed her real life.

Liz is one of the few people in the world to get close to rock's great enigma, Michael Jackson. And vice versa

At the Betty Ford Clinic, she had met and fallen for a young construction worker twenty years her junior. He was a completely nobody and the only thing that they remotely shared in common, on paper or anywhere else, was an interest in alcohol and a desire to beat it.

By April 1990 Liz's weight had ballooned to 15 stone. Her kidneys were shot to pieces by overuse of antibiotics and she was hospitalized for a fever and sinus infection. A week later, she was rushed to St John's hospital in Santa Monica. Doctors diagnosed a particularly virulent form of viral pneumonia and predicted that she was sinking fast. Liz was put on a life-support machine. Not for the first time the world's press issued hourly bulletins about the imminent death of Elizabeth Taylor. Again, front-page stories were displaced by her mortal illness. And once again, she found herself between a rock and a hard place. And, once more, she managed to survive the experience.

CHAPTER VI

LIZ IN LIMBO

Elizabeth Taylor wasn't overstating the matter when she made the candid admission: 'Everything was handed to me: looks, fame, wealth, honour, love. I rarely had to fight for anything. But I've paid for that luck with disasters: the deaths of so many good friends, terrible illnesses, destructive addictions, broken marriages. All things considered, I'm damned lucky to be alive.' If an inventory of her physical ailments was compiled, it would end up being the thickness of a respectable medical dictionary.

Not one of Liz's marriages has ever impeded this astonishing catalogue of mishaps. But it's no coincidence that her hardest personal battles – to beat drug and alcohol addiction – have been fought in the long shadow of the Betty Ford Clinic. Although 'incident prone', as Burton memorably put it, Liz's physical accidents were increasingly aggravated by her sundry addictions. They had once merely been the unlucky quirks of fate.

The most dramatic benefit of surviving viral pneumonia in 1990 was that it forced Liz to shed thirty pounds. This new reminder of her mortality also had a galvanizing effect on her private life and she felt the familiar desire to remarry. One can argue that this was simply a reaction to stave off the encroaching loneliness of an ageing Hollywood star á la Norma Desmond. The simple truth is that Liz needed someone around who would look after her: someone she could lean on, a support who would comfort as well as care for her. Liz has famously (and famously few) close friends like Michael Jackson, but the Jacksons of this world, though great on the phone, prefer to live in splendid isolation.

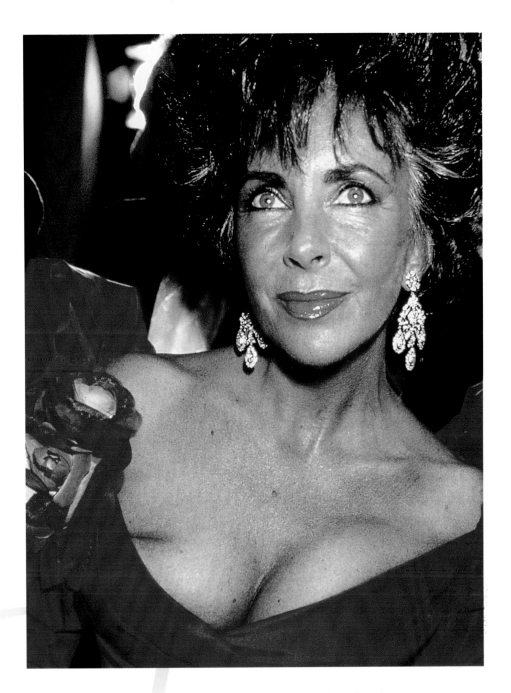

Simply the best: better than all the rest. Liz in rock 'n' roll mood

*Larry Fortensky had no idea what he was marrying into. He was a
big man physically, but he was well out of his depth in other senses*

Liz's unlikely knight turned out to be Larry Fortensky, that fellow inmate at the Betty Ford Clinic, who was desperately trying to patch up his own life. Larry wasn't just a companion to Liz: he was a minder, lapdog and eventually a lover. With his flowing golden locks, easy charm and brute good looks, Larry was a physically flattering escort. He was seemingly untouched by the dizzy proximity of so much wealth and, like Liz, he was desperately in need of someone who would keep him away from the demon sauce.

To say that Larry was a most unlikely fiancé for a seven-times married, legendary movie queen would be to put the case mildly. Fortensky grew up in Stanton, a no-nonsense, working-class suburb 60 miles south of Los Angeles. He was the eldest of seven children. A hard drinker since his teens, his attempts to make a career for himself as a trucker in the construction business had not been helped by his arrests, on at least two occasions, for drunken driving.

Following the last arrest, his local union branch decided to send him to a rehabilitation clinic. In 1988, an apprehensive Larry checked into the Betty Ford Clinic, where Liz had arrived a few days earlier. Although no one could accuse Larry of model citizenship, plenty of people in his home town still speak kindly of him. 'Believe it or not,' says his ex-wife Karin, 'Larry was just about the coolest guy in Orange County about 100,000 Heinekens ago.' Like several others, she remembers him as being honest, decent and funny.

Larry was also, as events would prove, surprisingly lucky. One of the Betty Ford rules forbids relationships between patients. However, under what were clearly fairly lax circumstances, the oddly-suited pair managed to find frequent consolation in each other's company. When Larry eventually checked out of the clinic, Elizabeth wrote wistfully in her diary: 'My favourite animal, Larry, has gone. I miss him terribly.' It was not for long. Liz stayed in touch with Larry, probably as much to her own surprise as his. When she left the clinic, they went on rambling dates to lonely places in her car. It's no secret that her friends and peers were less than enamoured of her new beau. In fact they were stingingly cynical. 'Liz is going out with the handyman,' was the casual and much bandied comment among the Beverly Hills set. But Liz persisted. In fact their affair, in many respects, was terribly romantic. A classic odd-couple scenario that any Hollywood studio would have been proud to dream up, package and then sell to a huge market that thrives on improbable love stories. The movie may yet be made.

One has to question the wisdom of the marriage itself. If Liz had left Larry to his own devices, and was happy enough with their clandestine relationship and mutual support, they might still be together today. They wanted to feel sure about each other. There was a lot to take on board, particularly for Larry. In the event, they were married three years later at Michael Jackson's Neverland estate at Rancho Mirage, California, amid the biggest blast of publicity that had accompanied a wedding since Prince Charles married Lady Diana Spencer. Their guest list was a who's who of fame and power in America: ex-President Ronald Reagan and his wife, Nancy, Frank Sinatra, Bob Hope, Liza Minnelli, Franco Zeffirelli, David Hockney, et al. The snob photographer, needless to say, was Herb Ritts. However, the Fortensky family was not so well represented. Routine investigations by security forces had unearthed a long list of police charges against some members of Larry's family, including a sixteen-month spell in jail for one of his relatives following a serious charge of reckless driving. There were ludicrous compromises. Larry's best man ended up being Liz's hairdresser, Jose Eber – hardly the sort of guy with whom Larry would shoot pool and shift a dozen (non-alcoholic) beers in the local bar.

The wedding ceremony itself, despite massive security, was nearly drowned out by fleets of hovering helicopters hired by TV companies and tabloid newspapers to attempt to photograph the event. Despite their joint tally of nine previous trips to the altar, the couple ambitiously promised to 'love each other more than we have ever loved before'. In a stunt they boasted of for weeks after, the *National Enquirer* even managed to get one of its reporters to skydive into the party. Before his feet touched the ground, he was caught and summarily ejected by platoons of armed guards. He was lucky to leave alive, let alone intact.

Back in Liz's Beverly Hills bubble, the married couple enjoyed an extended period of grace. If nothing else, the resulting publicity did no harm at all to sales of her latest perfume, 'White Diamonds', which would prove almost as lucrative as her first fragrance, 'Passion'. But the mismatch potential was already making its presence felt. In his recent biography of Liz Taylor, *Liz: An Intimate Biography Of Elizabeth Taylor* (Mandarin Paperbacks, 1996), C David Heymann depicted the couple as an inverted Henry Higgins and Eliza Dolittle. He suggests that their exquisite incompatibility was a huge turn-on for both of them. Liz arranged for Larry's teeth to be capped, she had his hair streaked, fed him gourmet meals and even paid for speech lessons. Larry insisted on continuing with his job in the construction business and Liz claims she made sandwiches for him every morning.

At first, Liz's defences seemed equal to the challenge. 'I've often thought of changing into a skimpy French maid's uniform,' she confided on Oprah Winfrey's show, 'renting a huge stretch limo and turning up at the construction site. I'd like to

Larry was infatuated with Liz, and she with him. But their disparate backgrounds would tear them apart

Liz and her mother Sara Taylor. Sara was possibly the greatest influence on Liz's life

see his face when I get out with trays of finger sandwiches and caviar. But I guess it would blow all his friends' minds.' On the same show Liz said her husband had helped her reclaim a childhood she had never had: 'The child in me was suppressed. It worked, it was paid, it was on the screen, but it was not me.'

However, the couple's marital bliss was not to last. Strange stories began to seep out from the Bel Air mansion where the last great screen star and the young construction worker lived with their parrots, paintings, diamonds and extensive collection of self-help manuals. One such tale was Liz's offer of $1 million to Larry if he could stop smoking. Other husbands might think the terms reasonable, but Larry reportedly told his wife: 'If I could, I would, but I can't. So you'll just have to live with it, won't you, dear?'

Liz rarely lived with anything she didn't want to for long. Under her exacting house rules, Larry was obliged to be teetotal, substance-free and permanently in touch with his karma. He lived mostly on salads, worked out daily and practically rattled with vitamins. His friends say that his last remaining pleasure was a snatched cigarette. Such was the vehemence of the ensuing row about his smoking that Larry checked into the Beverly Hills Ritz Carlton for a week.

Worse was to come when Larry's cousin, Sandra Souza, unhelpfully disclosed that the couple had taken to sleeping in separate bedrooms. On visits to his family, a raddled Larry explained that the new arrangements were necessary because Liz 'snored like a truck driver'. Needless to say, she had her own reasons. Following a number of hip replacements, she was not at all pleased by Larry's tendency to roll over in his sleep and boot her in the side. The symptoms of a marriage in decline are always the hardest to live with and during those years in limbo, Liz and Larry began to shrivel into their own routines.

Liz spent her mornings in her specially designed orthopaedic bed, talking on the phone to her friends. Larry, when not indulging his working-class fantasy of turning up at the building site, would sit on the couch eating crisps. At 1 p.m., Liz's therapist would arrive and only after that unmissable session did she join Larry for lunch in the exotic tropical garden that he contracted himself to build in the grounds of her house. On the rare occasions when Liz wasn't gossiping on the phone, she talked to her parrots, trying to school them unsuccessfully into plugging her perfumes. 'I love diamonds,' she cooed for months on end. The birds couldn't be teased into saying a single word.

Thwarted in her attempts to educate the parrots, Liz would spend the rest of the day watching TV soaps. At 4 p.m., tea would be served, English style – a habit of a lifetime. Then, at 5 p.m., Liz would change for dinner with Larry at 8 p.m. Once dinner was over, she would retire early. It was a small miracle that either of them kept their sanity.

Liz's mother, the redoubtable Sara Taylor, died aged 99 in September 1994. At the time, Liz's friend Michael Jackson was under investigation for child molestation. Although this was a period of intense grief for her, Liz found the energy to try to help salvage Jackson's mortally wounded credibility. The seriousness of the charges was never in doubt. Liz, drawing on a lifetime of real and imaginary scandals, persuaded Jackson to flee to London and seek counselling at a private clinic. Given that the British press are the most predatory in the world, this was akin to inviting a plucked chicken to roost in a baking oven.

With handkerchiefs flapping from his face like a Foreign Legion scarf put on back to front and his predilection for oxygen tents and toys, Jackson was the ripest target the press had focused on in years. He could not have found a more brilliant friend than Liz even if he had the temerity to invent one. Jackson, so out of touch with reality thanks to his enormous wealth and strange obsessions, was taking a huge gamble but Liz was one of the very few people who could understand the repercussions such a scandal would wreak on his monstrous fame – she'd lived it. When she announced that Michael was 'the least weird' person she knew, she was probably telling the truth. Jackson's trip to London was acutely embarrassing for him, but it scored serious points. The crucial tactic that Liz impressed on him was to face his accusers, and it worked. Jackson settled the matter in cash. The news hounds drifted off to fresher kills.

However, there was little that Liz could do to reinvigorate her marriage to Larry. The negative effects of their war of attrition were extremely visible. Liz's weight increased and the loose-fitting clothes she once sported in the 1980s came back out of the closet. The promotion of a new fragrance, 'Black Pearl', only seemed to advertise her weight gain to the millions of bewitched females who had bought into the marketing dreams of 'Passion' and 'White Diamonds'. But Liz anticipated the response quite magnificently. In February 1996 she stage-managed a quite brilliant marketing strategy by appearing in a string of her favourite soaps – *The Nanny*, *Can't Hurry Love*, *Murphy Brown* and *High Society* – as a deranged cameo of herself, looking for a mysterious gem which she pretended to have lost on location. It was an ingenious piece of advertising.

But it's a genuine pity Liz couldn't put that ingenuity to work on salvaging her marriage to Larry. She probably lost more than the highly publicized £1 million

*You could never blame or tame Liz. She always stuck by her
friends through thick and thin. Jackson paid her back in jewels*

One of Liz's most understated talents is how witty she is with the microphone

marriage settlement arranged with Fortensky's lawyers. Silence over a marriage such as theirs commands a far higher price. A lawyer was quoted as saying that Mr Fortensky would earn £3 million for a 'kiss and tell' book, doubled by film and TV rights. 'Larry may be simple,' continued the lawyer, 'but he is not stupid. Elizabeth is not stupid either.' Only the divorce lawyers and the divorced couple themselves know the exact figures that were agreed. However, legal sources reported that 64-year-old Liz offered a cash settlement of £5 million, £1.5 million in shares, a house worth £1.3 million, three Harley Davidson motorbikes, a limousine and £500,000 worth of jewellery and clothes. Did Larry deserve it? Probably, if only because their marriage lasted four years. Who's to say it couldn't have worked itself out if Liz and Larry weren't so much in the public eye?

Weeks later, just after the divorce had been formalized, Liz was rushed to hospital with a suspected heart attack. She was confined to bed and put on cardiac monitors after wild fluctuations in her blood pressure. Rumours circulated that she was suffering from a degenerative heart disease linked to her past addiction to painkillers. As Christa D'Souza solemnly noted in *The Sunday Times*: 'It is a sad, brittle end to what should have been a match made in heaven, made especially poignant by a comment the jubilant and skinny Taylor made just three years ago: "I love him for what he is, and he is devoted to me. He is not sophisticated or rich and powerful and his manners may be crude, but he gives me such peace, comfort and love." Up and down, up and down. Plus ça change, Liz.'

Chapter VII

In the Pink

op artist and social commentator Andy Warhol once said, when asked about the afterlife, 'It would be very glamorous to be reincarnated as a giant ring on Elizabeth Taylor's finger.' He was fantasizing, of course. But even in her sixties, Elizabeth evokes the kind of glamour that makes people want to genuflect. No other living movie star can inspire that sort of instinctive, awed respect. One saw that when she was awarded a fellowship at the fifty-first British Academy of Film and Television Awards in 1999. Star after star paid homage. Although there is no formal record, statement or certificate to that effect, Liz is the last of the great twentieth-century screen legends and she is cherished the world over for that fact alone.

One hack at her London press conference had the temerity to ask whether Liz was bored with being a legend. 'I don't feel like a legend,' she responded. 'A legend sounds like someone who is dead, and I don't feel dead.' It would have been all too easy for Liz to retire into royal seclusion, eking out her twilight years behind her massive security gates in Beverly Hills. But Liz, in every respect, has saved one of her most important roles for last.

For a decade and more, Liz has vociferously championed the fight against Aids: an epidemic which has devastated gay communities across the globe and set back health projects in the Third World by any number of years. Liz's involvement in the Aids cause is total. As the national chairman for America's leading Aids research organisation, AmFAR, she has had to testify before congressional committees and has appeared at many fund-raising benefits. 'That will never stop,' says Liz. 'That's

Liz was a fabulous piece of pop art. Andy Warhol famously painted her. But she was always bigger than any genre

The elusive Oscar: Liz picked up two of the most prized awards in motion pictures for
Best Actress in Butterfield 8 *and* Who's Afraid Of Virginia Woolf?

my twenty-four-hour-a-day job. There is so much to be done in education, support and research. I don't think people can think about it enough until a cure is found.'

The reasons why she is such a proven and effective campaigner have grown organically out of her own experience. As the one-time wife of a Republican senator (John Warner), Liz has first-hand knowledge of dealing with issues at the highest level. As an actress, she has an innate liberalism and instinctive hatred of bureaucracy; as a successful perfume tycoon, she has a hard nose for money, and finally, the fame and respect she commands for having lived her life so publicly has given her enormous power.

Liz has reinvented herself, not for the first time. 'I don't think of myself as an actress,' she said at the 1999 BAFTA awards, 'and I didn't think any of you did. Quite rightly too,' she told an audience comprising some of the biggest names in the British film industry. She makes an excellent point. Liz has grown far beyond any character she could be asked to play on screen. She has graduated from the world's most desirable woman into a political activist, and partly through that work, into one of the most influential gay icons of the twentieth century.

To assess the qualities required to be an icon, you need look no further than a list of other women who have played the role in the past: Judy Garland, Jackie Kennedy, Marilyn Monroe, Marlene Dietrich, Joan Crawford, Bette Davis, Liza Minnelli and the late Diana, Princess of Wales. All of these women combined fame, beauty and, to varying degrees, vulnerability, or a feeling for tragedy which renders them unusually sympathetic to a community beguiled by beauty and primed by prejudice. Liz has been a fully paid-up member for years.

From the very first moment that she embraced the Aids cause she established her credentials on a different and superior level. To have Aids, or to be HIV positive, is an illness; to be gay is not. Liz is not in the business of ignoring a life-threatening disease because the sufferers are, for the most part, homosexual. Experience has taught her to be fearless about her beliefs.

There is more to this involvement than mere identification. Liz has bought into the trappings and lived the role of the great screen diva – but she also has the scars. It can never be overstated how her intimacy with death has shaped her own views and, no less significantly, the gay community's perception of her. She has experienced deaths that have been as sudden and indiscriminate as the Aids epidemic itself. Liz has outlived four of her husbands: Mike Todd, Nicky Hilton, Michael Wilding and Richard Burton. In addition to her own relations, there was the tragic death of her long-time secretary, Roger Wall, who committed suicide rather than face the ravages of a long HIV illness. More hurtful still was the loss of her publicist, Chen Sam, who turned up to nurse Burton through a bout of malaria and ended up working for her for twenty years. Many of her best friends, including Montgomery Clift, Rock Hudson and Jimmy Dean – all either gay or bisexual actors – died before their time.

There have been long-term illnesses too. Her daughter-in-law, Aileen Getty, estranged wife of her son, Christopher Wilding, has had Aids since 1984. 'It seemed strangely ironic, after fighting the stigma involved with Aids for so many years, fighting for others, then to find my own daughter [in-law] was HIV positive,' said Liz when she found out. The news that Aileen had contracted the disease only became public knowledge during a fierce custody battle with Christopher Wilding. Although at the time Aileen claimed that she had caught the disease from an infected blood transfusion, she now avoids answering questions about how it happened. But Aileen has absorbed some of her mother-in-law's campaigning attitude. In 1997 she posed naked for a living art exhibition in Los Angeles to raise awareness of Aids, wearing a provocative sign that said: 'Please Touch'.

The irony is that Liz was absorbed into the gay lexicon long before she emerged as one of the gay community's most prolific and powerful spokespersons. Her appeal to the gay sensibility has been astonishing. Her excesses, bawdiness and her 'I don't give a damn' attitudes have been preparing the ground for this role since the 1950s. For years, Liz has been her own one-woman emporium of extraordinary kitsch tastes. She turned the big-hair beehive of the 1950s into the 1970s haystack; she ballooned from skin-tight, cleavage-revealing ensembles into giant, blowsy marquees. Her love of diamonds started a craze for diamanté. But it's as much about what she inspired as what she wore. Glitzy TV mini-series, such as *Dynasty* and *Dallas*, were modelled on her lifestyle. She and Richard Burton provided the original template for the rich behaving badly. Liz inspired Warhol to paint a series of silk screen prints, many of which now hang in Michael Jackson's Neverland estate. It's a hoary, over-used adage but if Liz didn't exist, someone would have had to invent her.

Liz's inexorable progression to becoming a gay icon was not entirely vicarious. Serendipity played its part. Her best work – by a long chalk – was in films by gay playwrights, who were forced to disguise their overtly homosexual themes. The most significant and brilliant of these was unquestionably Tennessee Williams. Liz was one of his greatest screen muses. The codes which these writers were forced to adopt to beat the censor were not wasted on her. She was as attuned to the gay subtext of *Cat On A Hot Tin Roof* as was any viewer with a modicum of sophistication. A cursory glance at her filmography (see pages 174–190) reveals that she has played

Mrs Shapari Khashoggi and Liz swap beauty tips after a Survive International Children rally in 1997

Rock Hudson was one of Liz's most memorable screen lovers. He was certainly one of her greatest friends. His death prompted her to fight a life-long battle for Aids awareness

a whole range of great screen bitches. Even in her most trashy movies, Liz contrived to generate the sort of camp inappropriateness that many gays find irresistible.

If one had to pick a turning point in Elizabeth Taylor's life – the moment when she changed from simply being a concerned star into someone who could use her fame to help others, it would have to be the death of Rock Hudson. Hudson was the first screen celebrity victim of Aids and the news of his condition horrified the world. Undeterred by the rumours about how Aids was spread, Liz kept a vigil by his side during the eight weeks that it took him to die. He finally passed away on 2 October 1985, a 90-pound husk of the 6' 4", muscle-bound matinee idol who bewitched a whole generation of women. His friends – and the press – were aghast.

In a forty-year career, Hudson made sixty-three films, ranging from westerns to musical comedies and epics. He contracted Aids in mid-1984, around the same time as Aileen Getty. After months of rumours about his illness, he authorized an announcement while he was having powerful drug treatment at a hospital in Paris. A week later, he returned to Los Angeles on a chartered flight, haggard and exhausted.

On 24 August Hudson discharged himself after doctors said they could do no more for him. In his last few months he received an enormous number of letters, flowers and messages from fans, as well as thanks from other Aids sufferers and from homosexual groups, who said his disclosure had helped them immeasurably. Liz organized an Aids benefit in his honour that raised a million dollars. Hudson was too ill to attend and shortly afterwards he died.

Despite the sympathy, Hudson was criticized by some actors, particularly those with whom he had worked during the filming of ten guest appearances on the TV series, *Dynasty*, for concealing his disease and putting their health at risk. However, many Hollywood stalwarts rallied around him, almost entirely because of Elizabeth Taylor's unprecedented support. He had been her co-star in *Giant* and, more importantly, was the proverbial rock when her own private life was in turmoil. The two had remained fast friends. Towards the end of his life, Hudson revealed how much he had suffered to live up to the swashbuckling, macho image of his films. For the last months of his life, the tabloids reported almost daily the debilitating details of his illness, his closet homosexuality and the unhappy marriage, which was typically arranged by Hollywood image-makers and predictably ended up in divorce after three years. Everything Hudson ever did became recast or reappraised in the light of the tragedy. It was the cruellest of goodbyes.

Hudson's death, and the subsequent tabloid witch-hunts which resulted in the houndings of Liberace, Freddy Starr, Derek Jarman, Malcolm Forbes (the super-rich publisher and Liz's bisexual lover), plus a legion of others, was a levelling lesson in the vulnerability of the rich and famous to the disease. For the first time since the Great Plague and two world wars, there was global fear in the ranks of the glitterati at the indiscriminate rampage of an incurable and invisible killer. Liz rose to the challenge with a nerve that many found difficult to credit.

It is embarrassing now to remember the mystery and terror which surrounded Aids from its first appearance in the early 1980s. In Britain it was marked by the tombstone TV advertisements financed by the government. In gay bars, used pint glasses were pointedly thrown in dustbins by bar staff whenever they suspected that a customer might be carrying the virus. There were articles in newspapers about how mosquitoes and barber-shop razors could spread the disease. Such was the fear and ignorance that those visiting the first dying Aids patients were swathed in plastic coating, with the horribly distinct apprehension that this was for the visitor's protection rather than the patient's. Meanwhile, there were grim stories of families rejecting their tragically affected children; of lovers spurning lovers; of petitions to turn people out of their flats or remove children from classrooms; of meals pushed under doors; of the burning of beds, linen and towels: in other words, there was a creeping general panic.

It was into this atmosphere of ignorance and fear that the late Diana, Princess of Wales, and Elizabeth Taylor so boldly stepped. Their compassion and concern, displayed unhysterically and with humour and composure, was the turning point in the public's perception and acceptance of the possibility, indeed the necessity, of living alongside Aids. Long before it was a fashionable cause, Liz appeared on the cover of *Vanity Fair* magazine in the 1980s, condom in hand, under the headline 'Liz Aid'. At that time no other Hollywood star wanted to get involved with people suffering from Aids for fear that their careers would be ruined by the association. Liz, however, has never laboured under that delusion. The resistance by Hollywood and the political powers-that-be in Washington to the Aids crisis had, until Liz's intervention, been almost Macarthyesque. Actors, writers and directors with first-hand knowledge of the disease found themselves consigned to the ghetto.

Liz, to her eternal credit, cashed her chips in. Her feisty, eloquent and implacable resolve to educate people about Aids is probably the work of which she is most proud, and for which many thousands will never forget her. It has been a relentless, highly effective campaign. Following the announcement of Hudson's death, President Reagan telephoned Liz to express his condolences and politicians suddenly lined up to raise more money to combat the disease. It was a welcome change of attitude, although Liz believes that the Bush administration put the cause back by another ten years and that Democrat President Clinton has been less than enthusiastic about financing more research.

In many respects, her fight could be simply interpreted as part of a longer battle against the invasive press. That's partly a truth but a blinkered one. What close observers miss is that her actions are typical of the woman who never could stand suffering, although she had suffered greatly in her own life. 'It's going to take a famous heterosexual woman dying before Aids gets the attention of the heterosexual community,' Liz once said, and she may still be right.

Educating people about the disease has been the staple in her strategy. 'People can't afford to be loose and casual any more,' she says. 'I think we have to learn to be damned careful, and hopping from bed to bed, well, I think it's really a thing of the past.' Liz is still struggling to convince people who are almost all compassioned-out. 'This straight, intellectual guy said to me, "Elizabeth, you are the expert on Aids. I know Aids can be transmitted heterosexually, but it's just through the rectum, isn't it?"

Liz and the multi-millionaire tycoon Malcolm Forbes start rumours about a new dangerous liaison

I called him an asshole! I said, "No, the vaginal juices, dear."' Liz is continually astonished by the ignorance: 'I mean, there wouldn't be a Hollywood if it weren't for homosexuals.' She's right, of course. All the most meaningful Hollywood product of her generation, and much of ours, would never have reached the screen if we hadn't been prepared to take the chance.

Liz's campaign nearly sank like the *Titanic* in 1997. A brain tumour was diagnosed just before her sixty-fifth birthday. True to style, she refused to have an operation to remove the tumour – the size of a golf ball – until the day after her party, which was crowned (for better or worse) by Michael Jackson's rendition of 'Happy Birthday'. But the legacy of the delicate four-hour operation that she underwent stunned the picture editors of every newspaper in the world. Gone were the flowing, raven locks. Shortly afterwards, Liz was seen in Turkey, sporting a spiky white crop of closely-shaven hair. With the determination that has been a hallmark of her middle age, she faced the cameras and said: 'I look like an axe-murderer's victim, but at least I have a reason to go

Liz dressed up like a Christmas tree in The Blue Bird *(1976), billed as the first Russo-American film project. History was made. The box office begged to differ*

shopping for scarves.' Her understated humour won the day. Liz later revealed that her illness first began with headaches and memory lapses before worsening. 'I also started dropping things,' she says. 'Drinking glasses would fall out of my hand. And sometimes I would feel disorientated, my mind sort of funny.' She admitted to 'sheer terror' when the tumour was diagnosed, but added: 'I never think of giving up, and I certainly never think of suicide. Christ, no! I love life. If the knife slips and I never wake up, I'll die knowing I've had an extraordinary life.'

Liz told *Life* magazine of her feeling of 'wild joy' when she woke up after the operation: 'I didn't die; I didn't have a stroke. They got the tumour, and I'm pretty sure they left all my marbles. I've still got a lot of living to do. The Fat Lady has not yet sung.' Liz has a hard-won sense of humour where trauma is concerned, only matched by an almost supernatural will to survive.

Concerns over prescription drugs still lingered, however. Not long after Liz's tumour operation, sources close to her family claimed she was lapsing back into familiar addictive habits, and that her children and closest friends wanted her to return to the Betty Ford Clinic. Yet again, she appeared to be fighting a losing battle with drugs. A year after leaving the Cedars-Sinai Medical Centre in Los Angeles, she was back in the same hospital for another crucial operation, this time on her back.

To many of her fans, the greying of Elizabeth Taylor must surely seem like the desecration of a national shrine. But to the lady herself, perhaps it's a relief to have her days of classic beauty safely behind her. Her friends are worried by her decline. To quote one source: 'Liz is still a star, but she knows she needs to work to stop herself turning into a relic.' She has not made a major movie in years. As she herself said, it's almost certainly because no studio can afford to pay her insurance premiums. Since the mid-1980s, Liz's screen life has been restricted to a number of walk-on cameos in popular TV soap operas and only the very occasional film, such as Brian Levant's slick Jurassic take on *The Flintstones* (1994). Typically, Liz agreed to do the movie not to salvage a fading career, but on condition that the gala opening of the film would be used to secure funds for her Aids charities. The other, more obvious reason is that she couldn't resist playing an irreverent tart, the fabulous Pearl Slaghoople, John Goodman's mother-in-law from hell. Liz's sense of humour will always, thankfully, be the most difficult thing about her to kill.

As the century ended, she was still toying with the idea of making a serious comeback. Rod Steiger, an old friend and once-rumoured lover, was reported in various newspapers to be trying to woo her back with a possible remake of *The Wizard Of Oz*. The idea sounds a little too wildly geriatric even for Liz to contemplate. In Steiger's remake, Liz would return to Oz as an ageing Dorothy to chew over old times with Steiger's Scarecrow. The mind boggles. There is also talk of Polygram, the Canadian-owned company behind *Four Weddings And A Funeral* and *Elizabeth*, seeking Liz's involvement in a remake of Oscar Wilde's 1895 masterpiece, *The Importance Of Being Earnest*.

This, at least, makes sense. The film-makers want to update Wilde's work, but only so far as the 1930s in order to prise the film out of the drawing room, yet still retain the fabulous costumes. Liz, her appetite whetted by Stephen Fry's performance as the Victorian playwright in the 1998 British hit, *Wilde*, would be sensational casting. One insider was quoted as saying: 'Liz would be perfect for Lady Bracknell. She would be powerful, exotic and sexy – a fresh take on a familiar character.' There's also the dry irony that it's considered to be one of the campest roles in stage history. Part of the temptation for Liz is that it's been one of the rites-of-passage for every great Dame – notably Edith Evans in Anthony Asquith's 1952 film, but memorably and most recently, Maggie Smith on stage.

But the most daring potential project is one that Liz's long-time agent, Robby Lantz, insists is a strong possibility. This is a remake of Ingrid Bergman's 1964 film, *The Visit*, based on a searing black comedy by Friedrich Dürrenmatt. The story tells how a millionairess returns to her impoverished home town, promising the entire population that they will be rich for life if they conspire to murder her ex-lover. Whether these intriguing offers will actually bear fruit, only time will tell.

Time will also test the fabric of Elizabeth Taylor's fame. It's difficult to imagine Hollywood without her, even if she continues to grace it only with her presence, rather than her roles. Like the movies themselves, she's grown up with us, as we have with her. Liz has been blessed and cursed by the fact that her entire life has been played out in a series of settings forever denied the fourth wall. She's had to progress from childhood to middle-age in the full glare of publicity and it hasn't always been a pretty sight. In this respect she is easily the most important character she has ever played. There are really few secrets about Liz to which the world hasn't already been privy. In spite of this, she has stepped beyond criticism into something far grander: myth. There's still hope that she may yet give us a few sensational old ladies on screen. I, for one, will never bet against it.

*Liz has always been a formidable campaigner. Marriage to John Warner,
a Republican senator, gave her a taste for politics and the microphone*

The greying of Liz Taylor will always be difficult to accept for her fans. That's why the lady turned platinum blonde

*Liz prepares for the 1999 BAFTAs where she picked up a highly
prestigious Academy Fellowship award for services to film*

FILMOGRAPHY

1942 **THERE'S ONE BORN EVERY MINUTE** directed by Harold Young. This is Liz Taylor's film debut, in which she plays the youngest member of an eccentric American family. It is only 59 minutes long and stars Hugh Hubert, Tom Brown, Peggy Moran and Gus Schilling. It was an utterly anonymous beginning to the young Liz's career, but it was a start.

1943 **LASSIE COME HOME** directed by Fred Wilcox. This is the first of the *Lassie* series and the film that not only established its canine heroine (of which there were a number of stunt-dogs and replacements) but also established Liz as one of the upcoming child stars of MGM during the early 1940s. Roddy McDowall played opposite her and remained a lifelong friend. Donald Crisp, who both appeared in and part-directed DW Griffith's *Birth Of A Nation*, led the cast, supported by Edmund Gwenn, Dame May Whitty, Elsa Lanchester (who went on to immortality in James Whale's *Bride Of Frankenstein*) and Nigel Bruce.

1944 **JANE EYRE** directed by Robert Stevenson. Liz was loaned out to Twentieth Century Fox for a minor role in Charlotte Brönte's eerie tale of doomed love on the Yorkshire Moors. Joan Fontaine and Orson Welles were the lovers.

THE WHITE CLIFFS OF DOVER directed by Clarence Brown. Another minor role in a World War I tearjerker, which features Irene Dunne, Alan Marshall, Roddy McDowall and Gladys Cooper.

*Throughout her career, Liz's image was carefully packaged by
MGM, who treated their young star as an indulgent parent would*

Beaming with promise: the young star with the most glittering future in showbiz

NATIONAL VELVET directed by Clarence Brown, from a novel by Enid Bagnold. Liz's first major hit. Here she stars as a little girl who has her heart set on winning the Grand National. It co-stars Mickey Rooney, Anne Revere (who won an Oscar for her supporting role), Donald Crisp, Angela Lansbury and Reginald Owen.

1946 **THE COURAGE OF LASSIE** directed by Fred Wilcox. Classic children's yarn about a collie, addled by the Second World War, who ends up rescuing Liz from all sorts of misadventures.

1947 **CYNTHIA** directed by Robert Z Leonard, based on a play by Vina Delmar. It was released in Britain as *The Rich Full Life*. Liz stars with George Murphy and Mary Astor.

LIFE WITH FATHER directed by Michael Curtiz, the brains behind the Errol Flynn swashbuckling epics. Clarence Day Junior's tribute to his stern philosophising father originated as a play by Howard Lindsay and Russell Crouse. The teenage Liz plays the intermittent love interest.

1948 **A DATE WITH JUDY** directed by Richard Thorpe from a screenplay by Dorothy Cooper and Dorothy Kingsley. Neat study of preppy youngsters maturing into teenagers. Liz mixed it with Wallace Beery, Jane Powell, Carmen Miranda, Robert Stack and most of the MGM repertory cast.

JULIA MISBEHAVES directed by Jack Conway, based on the novel, *The Nutmeg Tree* by Margery Sharp. Another coming-of-age movie, with Walter Pidgeon, Greer Garson, Peter Lawford, Cesar Romero and Nigel Bruce.

1949 **LITTLE WOMEN** directed by Mervyn LeRoy. A remake of the Louisa May Alcott novel, previously filmed with Katharine Hepburn by George Cukor in 1933. Liz stars with June Allyson, Peter Lawford, Mary Astor, Janet Leigh and Margaret O'Brien. It was filmed in vivid Technicolor by Franz Planer, who was nominated for an Oscar.

CONSPIRATOR directed by Victor Saville, based on the novel by Humphrey Slater. Liz plays an innocent young wife who finds out that her husband is a commie spy. Pure McCarthyism and part of the late 1940s Cold War paranoia. With Robert Taylor, Robert Fleming, Harold Warrender and Marie Nay.

1950 **FATHER OF THE BRIDE** directed by Vincente Minnelli, based on the novel by Edward Streeter. Spencer Tracy steals this movie as the bewildered father coping very badly with his daughter's (Liz Taylor) marriage. Delightful support from Joan Bennett, Don Taylor and Leo G Carroll.

THE BIG HANGOVER written and directed by Norman Krasna. Liz falls for a lawyer (Van Johnson) whose allergy to strong drink threatens to sink his career. She reveals her maternal mettle in this comedy, which has little going for it apart from her effortless screen charm.

1951 **QUO VADIS?** directed by Mervyn LeRoy. The film was the highest grosser for MGM after *Gone With The Wind*. Liz plays a small role (uncredited) in this historical epic which features Robert Taylor, Deborah Kerr and Peter Ustinov as Nero. Another uncredited role was filled by Sophia Loren.

FATHER'S LITTLE DIVIDEND directed by Vincente Minnelli. A rather weak follow-up to *Father Of The Bride*, with Liz as the pregnant wife and Spencer Tracy regrooving his grumpy role as her father.

A PLACE IN THE SUN directed by George Stevens, based on Theodore Dreiser's novel, *An American Tragedy*. A great movie, with Liz delivering her first blisteringly sexual screen role. With Montgomery Clift and Shelley Winters. The film won six Oscars, including one for Stevens as director.

CALLAWAY WENT THATAWAY directed by Norman Panama and Melvin Frank. Howard Keel plays an old western star in this comedy which was intended to send up old Hollywood traditions. Liz is one of a bunch of MGM stars hired to play cameos. Released in Britain as *The Star Said No*.

1952 **LOVE IS BETTER THAN EVER** directed by Stanley Donen. This has been described as one of Liz's 'luscious' performances in which she becomes romantically involved with an artist's manager. Co-starring Tom Tully, Josephine Hutchinson and Larry Parks, who was later black-listed during the McCarthy witchhunts.

IVANHOE directed by Richard Thorpe. A screenplay by Noel Langley and Agnes Mackenzie, loosely inspired by Sir Walter Scott's novel. This was Liz's first major

On the set of Little Women, *a remake of the Louisa May Alcott novel, filmed in 1949*

movie to be shot in Britain. She plays a young Jewess who is about to be burnt at the stake until she is rescued by Robert Taylor's dashing knight. An MGM spectacular with George Sanders, Emlyn Williams and Finlay Currie.

1953 **THE GIRL WHO HAD EVERYTHING** directed by Richard Thorpe. Liz plays a young spoilt rich bitch who falls in love with one of her crooked father's clients. With William Powell, Fernando Lamas and Gig Young.

1954 **RHAPSODY** directed by Charles Vidor. Liz plays another wealthy young wench who falls in love with two musicians. With Vittoria Gassman, John Ericson and Louis Calhern.

ELEPHANT WALK directed by William Dieterle, based on a novel by Robert Standish. Liz plays the bored wife of a colonial tea plantation owner (Peter Finch) in Ceylon. The elephants stole the movie.

*Sharing the wheel with James Dean, Liz's friend and co-star in the sprawling
George Stevens' epic,* Giant. *Dean died in a carcrash soon after the film wrapped*

BEAU BRUMMELL directed by Curtis Bernhardt, based on a play by Clyde Fitch. An anti-royal film chosen perversely for the Royal Command Performance in front of the Queen. Liz Taylor and Stewart Granger steam away romantically, but Peter Ustinov walks off with the movie as the caddish Prince of Wales, ably supported by Robert Morley as Richard III.

THE LAST TIME I SAW PARIS directed by Richard Brooks from a screenplay he wrote with Julius and Philip Epstein, based on a novel by F Scott Fitzgerald. Liz plays an American girl who becomes involved with a writer (Van Johnson) who is corrupted by the capitalist system.

1956 **GIANT** directed by George Stevens, based on the massive novel by Edna Ferber. A real soap opera of an epic set in Texas from the turn-of-the-century up to the oil boom in the 1950s. Liz puts in a great performance (Oscar nominated) as a young virgin who ages into the most glamorous grandmother in film history. Rock Hudson plays her flinty husband. But the film will always be remembered for James Dean's last performance. His tough-as-nails character, Jett Rink, was the inspiration (if one can call it that) behind JR in the television series, *Dallas*. Dean died in a car crash just days after the movie was made.

1957 **RAINTREE COUNTRY** directed by Edward Dmytryk, based on the novel by Ross Lockridge. Liz plays a southern belle who falls in love with a young idealist, Montgomery Clift, during the American Civil War. With Eva Marie Saint, Lee Marvin and Nigel Patrick.

1958 **CAT ON A HOT TIN ROOF** directed by Richard Brooks, based on the cracking pot-boiler by Tennessee Williams, though considerably toned down for the screen. Liz, again nominated for an Oscar for her portrayal as Maggie the Cat, plays the wife of a bitter and twisted husband (Paul Newman) who refuses to sleep with her. Burl Ives puts in a cracking performance as Big Daddy, the plantation owner, whose offspring are too scared to tell him that he's dying of cancer. The death of Liz's husband, Mike Todd, in a plane crash just as shooting began, nearly unhinged her. The work she put into this performance saved her from total breakdown.

1959 **SUDDENLY LAST SUMMER** directed by Joseph L Mankiewicz, based on the play by Tennessee Williams, screenplay by Gore Vidal. Deeply spooky film in which Liz plays a young woman who is used to attract young boys for her predatory homosexual cousin. Montgomery Clift plays the psychiatrist, with Katharine Hepburn as the witch-like aunt. Clift nearly died in a car-crash during the making of this film. Both Liz and Hepburn were nominated for Oscars.

1960 **SCENT OF MYSTERY** (AKA **HOLIDAY IN SPAIN**) directed by Michael Anderson. A mystery that relied on a gimmicky odour being released in the cinema during certain points of the film. It never worked properly. Liz played a cameo role.

BUTTERFIELD 8 directed by Daniel Mann, based on a novel by John O'Hara. Liz won her first Oscar as Best Actress for her portrayal of a free-wheeling, nymphomaniac call girl. She hated the film, calling it sleazy and cheap. Her near death in real life almost certainly influenced a sympathy vote. With Laurence Harvey, Mildred Dunnock, Dina Merrill and Liz's new husband, Eddie Fisher.

1963 CLEOPATRA directed by Joseph L Mankiewicz. One of the most extraordinary films ever shot, thanks entirely to what was happening off-screen between Richard Burton and Liz Taylor, rather than the sludgy historical epic on screen. Rex Harrison played Caesar.

THE VIPS directed by Anthony Asquith, from a screenplay by Terence Rattigan. Richard Burton plays an Aristotle Onassis tycoon, who is importuned at a fog-bound London Airport by Maggie Smith. Liz plays Burton's wife, who is about to elope with a lover (Louis Jourdan). With Margaret Rutherford (who won an Oscar for Best Supporting Actress), Rod Taylor and Orson Welles.

1965 THE SANDPIPER directed by Vincente Minnelli, from a script by Dalton Trumbo and Michael Wilson. Liz plays a bohemian artist living in luxury on a Californian beach. Richard Burton is the teacher who takes charge of her illegitimate child. Stilted romance with Eva Marie Saint, Charles Bronson and Robert Webber.

1966 WHO'S AFRAID OF VIRGINIA WOOLF? directorial debut film for Mike Nichols, based on Edward Albee's superb play. Liz won her second Oscar for Best Actress for her portrayal of the drunken, rampaging wife of Richard Burton's history professor. It's Liz's favourite film of her own work. Many speculated about whether the on-screen showdowns were happening off-screen too. With George Segal and Sandy Dennis (who won the Oscar for Best Supporting Actress).

1967 THE TAMING OF THE SHREW directed by Franco Zeffirelli, lifted from Shakespeare's eponymous play. An excellent period piece, again something of a classic, and one of Zeff's finest films. Burton plays the scheming suitor, Petruchio, who brings Liz's shrewish merchant's daughter to heel. With Michael York, Alfred Lynch, Cyril Cusack and Michael Hordern.

DOCTOR FAUSTUS directed by Richard Burton and Neville Coghill, from the play by Christopher Marlowe. Burton starred as the lusty doctor who makes a pact with the Devil in a student production of the play at Oxford. Here he plays Mephistopheles. Liz makes a silent cameo as Helen of Troy.

REFLECTIONS IN A GOLDEN EYE directed by John Huston, based on the novel by Carson McCullers. Liz plays a major's wife who discovers that her husband has latent

A shoulder to cry on: Liz and Paul Newman in Cat On A Hot Tin Roof, *the landmark movie that Liz made while still grieving for her third husband, Mike Todd*

An Oscar at last: Laurence Harvey sweet-talks Liz in one of her least favourite films, Butterfield 8. But it won Liz her first Academy Award for Best Actress

homosexual tendencies. Marlon Brando plays the Major. With Julie Harris, Brian Keith and Robert Forster.

THE COMEDIANS directed by Peter Glenville, from a screenplay by Graham Greene, based on his own novel about Englishmen caught up in a Haitian dictatorship (presumably Papa Doc). Liz co-stars with Richard Burton, Alec Guinness, Peter Ustinov and Lilian Gish.

1968 **BOOM!** directed by Joseph Losey from a screenplay by Tennessee Williams based on his play *The Milk Train Doesn't Stop Here Any More*. Liz plays the reclusive Mrs Goforth, with Noel Coward as the equally eccentric neighbour. Richard Burton arrives as the angel of death. A bizarre piece.

SECRET CEREMONY directed by Joseph Losey, based on a short story by Marco Denevi. Losey's most self-indulgent film features Liz, Robert Mitchum, Mia Farrow and Peggy Ashcroft.

1970 **THE ONLY GAME IN TOWN** directed by George Stevens, based on a play by Frank D Gilroy. Liz plays a chorus girl in Las Vegas (though the film was shot in a Paris studio so she could be near Richard Burton). Warren Beatty plays a compulsive gambler. He turned down an enormous number of movies and took a modest fee just for the chance of acting with Liz.

1972 **UNDER MILK WOOD** directed by Andrew Sinclair, from a screenplay he adapted from Dylan Thomas's irreverent tome. Liz was given little choice but to appear in this vehicle with Richard Burton who was mad about the poet. Peter O'Toole, Glynis Johns, Vivien Merchant and Sian Phillips also appeared.

ZEE & CO. (AKA **X, Y AND ZEE**) directed by Brian G Hutton from a screenplay by Edna O'Brien. Liz stars as the wife of an adulterous, successful architect and seeks out a perverse revenge. She ends up in bed with Susannah York. With Michael Caine, Margaret Leighton and John Standing.

HAMMERSMITH IS OUT directed by Peter Ustinov, script by Stanford Whitmore. A bizarre black comedy, based on the Faust legend, in which a homicidal mental patient (Richard Burton) escapes and becomes the most influential man in the country.

Liz aids and abets his cause, but despite the added pickle of Ustinov and Beau Bridges, this cannot be ranked among the world's greatest nut-house movies.

1973 **NIGHT WATCH** directed by Brian G Hutton, based on the play by Lucille Fletcher. A tired, old-fashioned thriller. Liz plays a woman recovering from a nervous breakdown, who sees dead bodies in the boarded-up house across the garden. With Laurence Harvey, Billie Whitelaw and Tony Britton.

DIVORCE HIS/DIVORCE HERS (TV movie) directed by Waris Hussein, script by John Hopkins. One of the more ghastly coincidences in Liz's movie career. As she and Richard Burton were falling out of love, this two-part drama seemed to mimic and mock them on screen. It's the last time they worked together on a film.

ASH WEDNESDAY directed by Larry Peerce, based on a script by Jean-Claude Tramont. Liz plays a middle-aged woman who goes to Switzerland for plastic surgery so that she can look younger for her husband, Henry Fonda. With Keith Baxter and Helmut Berger.

THE DRIVER'S SEAT (AKA **IDENTIKIT**) directed by Guiseppe Patroni Griffi. Liz plays a spinster who meets a murderer and finds her past neuroses catching up with her as she falls in love. With Ian Bannen and Mona Washbourne.

1974 **THAT'S ENTERTAINMENT** Liz narrates, while a compilation of MGM musicals floats over the screen. With Fred Astaire, Gene Kelly, Bing Crosby, Peter Lawford, Liza Minnelli, Debbie Reynolds, Frank Sinatra, Mickey Rooney and James Stewart.

1976 **THE BLUE BIRD** directed by George Cukor. The first major USA–USSR co-production is a glitzy, desperately pedestrian version of Maeterlinck's delicate fantasy about two kids and their quest for the blue bird of happiness. Liz stars with Jane Fonda, Ava Gardner, Cicely Tyson, Harry Andrews and Robert Morley.

VICTORY AT ENTEBBE (TV movie) directed by Marvin J Chomsky, screenplay by Ernest Kinoy. Seat-clutching action movie that enjoyed some acclaim because of its star-studded cast. With Helmut Berger, Richard Dreyfuss, Linda Blair, Kirk Douglas, Anthony Hopkins and Burt Lancaster.

Noel Coward, Richard and Liz on the set of Boom!, *a bizarre conflation of two works by Tennessee Williams: a Broadway flop,* The Milk Train Doesn't Stop Here Any More, *and a story,* Man Take This Up Road

1978 **A LITTLE NIGHT MUSIC** directed by Harold Prince, based on his own Broadway production of Stephen Sondheim's musical. Liz gets to sing the best- known song, 'Send In The Clowns', in this piece about adult relationships. With Diana Rigg, Len Cariou, Hermione Gingold and Lesley-Anne Down.

RETURN ENGAGEMENT (TV movie) directed by Joseph Hardy, screenplay by James Prideaux. Liz mistakenly cast as an ancient history professor who falls for an angst-ridden student. A low point in her career.

1979 **WINTER KILLS** written and directed by William Richert, based on a novel by Richard Condon. A plump Liz made a cameo appearance in this heavy-going melodrama in which the brother of an assassinated president tracks down the killers.

Liz drank and swore her way to her second Oscar in Mike Nichols' searing production of Edward Albee's Who's Afraid Of Virginia Woolf? *George Segal gleefully watches from the sofa.*

Shades of a JFK conspiracy, but the movie sank despite a glittering cast that included Jeff Bridges, John Huston and Anthony Perkins.

1980 **THE MIRROR CRACK'D** directed by Guy Hamilton from a screenplay by Anthony Shaffer, and inspired by one of Agatha Christie's *Miss Marple* stories. A camp but highly enjoyable murder mystery that sees Liz's ageing prima donna square up to Kim Novak's rising star. Poison is in the air ... and in the drinks. With Angela Lansbury as Miss Marple, Rock Hudson as the director and Tony Curtis as the sleazy agent.

1981 **GENOCIDE** directed by Arnold Schwartzman. A documentary about the Holocaust narrated by Liz and Orson Welles, and scripted by Schwartzman, Martin Gilbert and Rabbi Marvin Hier.

Beauty and the beast: Liz and Marlon Brando smoulder in Reflections In A Golden Eye

1983 BETWEEN FRIENDS (AKA **NOBODY MAKES ME CRY**) (TV movie) directed by Lou Antonio. Liz, Carol Burnett and Barbara Bush get drunk, talk about sex and, in Liz's case, express the absolute need for a man to rule her. In reality, very few were able to do so.

1985 MALICE IN WONDERLAND (TV movie) directed by Gus Trikonis. Liz plays a spiky Hollywood gossip, Louella Parsons, to Jane Alexander's infamous Hedda Hopper. Witty, camp comedy about the Hollywood golden era.

NORTH AND SOUTH (TV movie) directed by Richard Heffron. Liz makes a special guest appearance in this sweeping, melodramatic soap opera about the Civil War. She was paid an astonishing $100,000 to appear.

1986 THERE MUST BE A PONY (TV movie) directed by Joseph Sargent, screenplay by Mart Crowley, based on a novel by James Kirkwood. A surprisingly sharp film, where Liz yet again plays a troubled screen star attempting a comeback after mental illness. Liz-watchers will relish the resonances of multiple marriages and an ex-husband who beat her. Robert Wagner and Mickey Rooney (playing himself) spice up the charmers and cads.

1987 POKER ALICE (TV movie) directed by Arthur Allan Seidelman. Liz and George Hamilton, the man she was rumoured to be stepping out with at the time, play a couple of gambling sharks in a Wild West town. Pure hokum.

1988 YOUNG TOSCANINI (AKA **IL GIOVANE TOSCANINI**) directed by Franco Zeffirelli, from a screenplay by William H Stadiem. An overblown romantic melodrama about the young composer's life. Liz plays Nadina Bulichoff. Co-stars C Thomas Howell, Sophie Ward, Pat Heywood, John Rhys-Davies and Franco Nero.

1989 SWEET BIRD OF YOUTH (TV movie) directed by Nicholas Roeg, screenplay by Gavin Lambert, from a play by Tennessee Williams. Liz plays the fading movie star Alexandra Del Lago who ensnares a young buck (Mark Harmon) to perpetuate her fantasy of glitter and youth.

1994 THE FLINTSTONES directed by Brian Levant, based on the strip cartoon. Liz plays the mother-in-law from hell, Pearl Slaghoople, in this rather frothy, fun, tongue-in-cheek look at downtown Los Angeles circa 5000 BC. With John Goodman, Rick Moranis, Elizabeth Perkins, Rosie O'Donnell, Kyle MacLachlan and Halle Berry.

The last of the great Hollywood legends: Liz in Cat On A Hot Tin Roof, *clinging to the bedposts.*
Why she never won an Oscar for this performance is one of the great mysteries and crimes of motion pictures

PICTURE CREDITS

Alpha:13,27,28,52,60,64,68,83,87,88,92,109,125,129,130,138,145,164,189, Alpha/angeli:167
Camera Press/Bob Penn: 76, Camera Press/Sam Levin: 98, Camera Press/Alan Davidson: 137,
Camera Press/Kip Rano: 151, Camera Press/Ian Lloyd: 173, Camera Press/Ray Hamilton: 188
Colour Library International: 91, Corbis: 32,33
Hulton Getty: 40,44,56,79,80,106,110,113,114,118,122,134, Hulton Getty/Sherman: 97, Hulton
Getty/G. Stroud: 117, Hulton Getty/McKenzie: 144,152
Pictorial Press: 6,9,15,16,19,23,24,30,35, 36,39,43,47,48,51,55,59,63,67,71,72, 75,93,95,101,102,
105,121,126,127,137, 142,147,155,163,168,171,175,176,187,191, Pictorial/Zuma/Sinbran: 172
Retna: 29, Retna/Steve Granitz: 10,148,156,160, Retna/Holland: 20,84,179, Retna/
Barry Talesruck: 133, Retna/Walter McBride: 141, Retna/Neal Preston: 159, Retna/Lux: 180,
Retna/Photofest: 183,184

The author and publishers have made every reasonable effort to contact all copyright holders. Any errors that may have
occurred are inadvertent and anyone who for any reason has not been contacted is invited to write to the publishers so
that a full acknowledgement may be made in subsequent editions of this work.

BIBLIOGRAPHY

The following titles offer an exhaustive and conclusive overview of Elizabeth Taylor's career to date:
Sheridan Morley: Elizabeth Taylor (Pavilion Books Ltd, 1998)
Alexander Walker: Elizabeth (Orion Books Ltd, 1997)
Donald Spoto: Elizabeth Taylor (Warner Books 1995)
David Thomson: A Biographical Dictionary of Film (André Deutsch Ltd, 1995)
C. David Heymann: Liz: An Intimate Biography of Elizabeth Taylor (Mandarin, 1996)
Kitty Kelly: Elizabeth Taylor: The Last Star (Michael Joseph, 1981)
Melvyn Bragg: Richard Burton: A Life (Little, Brown and Company, 1988)
The Macmillan International Film Encyclopedia (Third Edition, Macmillan)
Time Out Film Guide (Penguin)

SOURCES

BFI Library Services. Vanity Fair, Esquire, Films Magazine, Premiere, Time Out, The
Motion Picture Guide, Daily Express, Daily Mail, Daily Record, Daily Telegraph, Evening Standard,
the Guardian, the Independent, Independent On Sunday, The LA Times, Mail On Sunday, The
Mirror, The New York Times, The Observer, The People, The Radio Times, The Sun, Sunday
Correspondent, Sunday Telegraph, The Sunday Times, The Times, The Washington Post,
You Magazine